INSIDE THE

creative studio

INSPIRATION AND IDEAS FOR YOUR ART AND CRAFT SPACE

CATE COULACOS PRATO

INTERWEAVE
interweave.com

contents

4 INTRODUCTION

6 CHAPTER 1 | **A ROOM OF ONE'S OWN**

8 **Claim Your Creative Space** · MARY HETTMANSPERGER

12 **A Dream Studio Realized** · GINNY BURDICK

16 **In Her Shoes** · CATHERINE THURSBY

20 **Branching Out** · MARGIE WOODS BROWN

24 **Hay Loft to Artist's Loft** · SARA LECHNER

28 *Inspiration: An interview with Eva Hanusova*

30 CHAPTER 2 | **ORGANIZATION AND STORAGE**

32 **Clutter Out, Creativity In** · LESLEY RILEY

36 **Disarray to Display** · GINA LEE KIM

40 **Made to Order** · JANE DÁVILA

46 **Holtz Everything** · TIM HOLTZ

50 **Fits to a T** · RENAY LEONE

54 *Inspiration: 101 Organization and Storage Tips*

62 CHAPTER 3 | **FLEA MARKET FLAIR**

64 **From Dump to Divine** · BRENDA BRINK

68 **Top Drawer** · WENDY VECCHI

72 **A Little Jewel Box** · HOLLY A. STINNETT

76 **Nifty, Thrifty** · LUCIE SUMMERS

80 **Organizing with Vintage Collectibles** · SUSAN BORGEN

82 *Inspiration: An Interview with Elsie Flannigan*

84   CHAPTER 4 | SMALL SPACE, BIG STYLE

86   **In a Nutshell** · JANICE AVELLANA

90   **Room of Requirement** · LIZA JULIEN

94   **The Love Shack** · ROBERTA L. PHILBRICK

98   **Studio in the Sky** · SETH APTER

102   **Strategic Design** · MICHELLE SPAW

106   *Inspiration: An Interview with Gail Schmidt*

108   CHAPTER 5 | THE POWER OF LIGHT AND COLOR

110   **Let the Sunshine In** · LESLIE REGO

114   **Living in Color** · JUDITH CONTENT

120   **Yummy Goods** · MELISSA AVERINOS

124   **For Your Illumination** · BARBARA DELANEY

130   *Inspiration: My Blue Heaven* · KATHY YORK

132   CHAPTER 6 | MAKE IT YOUR OWN

134   **Extreme Studio Makeover** · POKEY BOLTON

140   **Drawn to Design** · KRISTIN KRAUSE

144   **Weaving Happiness** · CHRIS ERICKSON

148   **Sun & Fun** · JENNIFER HEYNEN

152   **A Window to Design** · CATHERINE NICHOLLS

156   *Inspiration: An Interview with Holly Berube*

159   RESOURCES

INSIDE THE CREATIVE STUDIO

INTRODUCTION

Do you dream of having a studio of your own, a place where you can think, create, make a mess, or even teach?

Maybe you have grand plans for a spacious room outfitted with big north-facing windows, huge tables for spreading out your supplies, and even a sink for rinsing out brushes or dyeing fabric. Perhaps you long for a cozy nook where you can play with your materials whenever you like without having to put everything away—a creative oasis amid the demands of family and day jobs.

Whether you have the resources to hire an architect and a crew to build the studio of your dreams or you just have four square feet to call your own, *Inside the Creative Studio* will give you the inspiration and ideas you need to make your dream come true.

The artists who have opened their studio doors to you in this collection come from all walks of life and areas of art. Some make a living selling what they create. For others, creating is a pastime they can't live without. Their studios range from freestanding, fully equipped showplaces to spare bedrooms turned into creative havens to closets outfitted as craft rooms—and everything in between.

Some artists like their studios neat and tidy; others thrive on a jumble of textures and colors. Some haunt flea markets and fill their creative spaces with vintage finds. Others like their environment to be sleek, modern, and spare.

What makes a good studio? At minimum, a studio is any place that inspires you and allows you to work on your art or craft in a safe and efficient manner. If you're a knitter, you may just need a comfy couch and baskets full of yarn. If you like to draw, a sketchpad, a light source, and your pencils may suffice. Quilters and assemblage artists tend to need space to spread out and different kinds of light sources.

Every studio in this book is different, and yet they all have one thing in common: they meet the needs of the artist who works and plays there.

And one other thing: they were all chosen for their potential to inspire you to create the studio you've always wanted.

CATE COULACOS PRATO
Studios magazine editor

chapter 1

"As I ascend the stairs to my studio, I leave the hustle and bustle of the world behind and enter a creative wonderland."

— MARGIE WOODS BROWN

A ROOM OF ONE'S OWN

Not for nothing did Virginia Woolf state that to be creative, a woman needs a room of her own. Even today, when many women have their own incomes, a room dedicated to pursuing one's creative passions can be hard to come by. It isn't always a matter of not having the square footage either. While men have always had their workshops and garages, women tend to think of a space dedicated to their creativity as an indulgence.

That's why having a studio is so important to any artist's life: by virtue of its existence, a studio proclaims that your creative life exists, and it matters.

Is it any wonder, then, that artists use words such as "sanctuary," "haven," and "dream come true" to describe their studios? They've recognized that their creativity is sacred and deserves its own space. Learn from the artists in the pages that follow how they got their studios and how you can get a room of your own, too.

claim your creative space

by MARY HETTMANSPERGER

peru, indiana

Having been an artist for most of my life, I have learned that one of the most important aspects of tapping into creativity is having an inspiring space to work in. This does not mean that I have always had the luxury of working in a fabulous studio. I have worked on my lap, at the kitchen table, in my basement, at many a tennis match watching kids play, and in a downtown studio loft.

maryhetts.com

In every case, changing spaces, moving, evolving, and growing have brought new adventures, challenges, and ideas for that ultimate studio space. The benefit to working in temporary places was that it allowed me to have a constant change of scenery and stimuli. But of course, the downfalls were many.

When it finally came time to build and create my studio space, I felt I was sincerely ready and glad I had not done it any sooner. Having a variety of studio experiences gave me time to really decide where I was going to build and what I wanted and needed. Much like my artwork, my concept of what I wanted in a studio evolved, and when it came time to build, the requirements had also changed.

So I began. I started by finding a local contractor who would work from my drawings. I wanted an all-metal building on a concrete slab. This type of building made the project very affordable, and the building would be easy to maintain. After having my studio in a loft downtown for several years, I knew I did not want

top right: Mary on the set of *Quilting Arts TV* with host and *Quilting Arts* editorial director Pokey Bolton.

below right: Black siding gives Mary's studio an artistic look.

MARY'S STUDIO

PHOTOS BY STEVE MANN

MARY'S
TIPS AND HINTS:

Considerations and needs for my ultimate studio space:

1 Cost

2 Use of my design and ideas

3 Easy maintenance

4 All one level

5 "Green" and efficient

6 Good light without losing wall space

7 Healthy work environment

8 Inspiring and unique

any stairs in my studio. Because we built it on our farm, I was able to spread out on one level and didn't have to pay extra for the land. My husband and I did a lot of the work ourselves, and I hired local subcontractors, saving even more money. I wanted the studio to be as "green" as possible, so that was a consideration in how I approached many aspects of the space. Simple things were important, such as adding a two-flush toilet and placing the main lighting windows high on the walls to allow me to have light without losing wall space. The ceilings are ten feet high with extra insulation in the walls and ceiling. I have open ductwork to avoid any heat/air loss and use an electric heat pump to save energy. Eventually, my plan is to supplement the power by adding windmills.

Open ductwork prevents heat and air loss.

The windows and doors were all purchased at a big-box hardware store, and I checked with them before I began for any returns and misorders that they might have had "in the back." Sure enough, they had several windows that had been ordered wrong and were returned. I was able to purchase these windows for one-third the original cost and could easily change my design to fit the windows.

I also saved money by checking with salvage yards, antique stores, and resale shops for doors, framing, cabinets, and so on.

My metalworking room has an exhaust system to maintain healthy air quality. I had my built-in shelving made by a local craftsman and decided not to stain or paint the wood, as I love the natural look. I finished off part of the studio in linoleum and part in a heavy,

durable carpet to avoid heat loss through the cement floor. Our home is not too far from the studio, and one concern was that the studio would look like another home: I wanted the building to have a unique and artistic look. So, I had the builder side the exterior with black siding, and surprisingly it does not get too hot in the summer. Also, the shape is distinctive, giving it the artistic look I was after. I am adding beautiful gardens and landscaping as time and money permit.

I think for me my patience paid off. I realize that what I thought I wanted twenty, fifteen, even ten years ago, is different than what I have now in my studio. Age, maturity, and even my artwork, dictated the direction in which the studio evolved. I am very fortunate to be in an amazing environment doing what I have a passion for. ✳

a dream studio
REALIZED

an old barn becomes a sleek art space

by **GINNY BURDICK**

coarsegold, california

My studio is the product of a wild dream—and of disciplined planning. When my husband and I first moved into our house in the foothills of the Sierras, the long-neglected barn on the hill reminded us of a promise we had made: someday, we would have an art studio.

ginnyburdick.com

We began collecting ideas: a box of magazine photos, catalogs, ideas jotted onto notebook paper, photos of studios we had visited, sketches and more sketches. For more than ten years, that box kept filling. Periodically, we would weed through it, discard some things, add new ones, and make additional notes.

Often, the dream seemed remote: the barn was a mess. It had been a working barn many years ago, then was converted to a series of very rustic meeting rooms by a previous owner. The building had good "bones"—all open strut work; old shop lights; a broken, yet strong concrete floor; and heavy wooden doors that blocked out the light. There were also happy memories of our sons who played in bands that rocked the walls and shook the strong wooden beams.

Over time, the dream expanded and grew as we began to define our needs carefully: the "dream" should include offices, a guesthouse, ample storage, a work

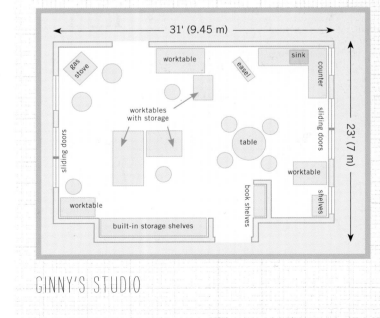

GINNY'S STUDIO

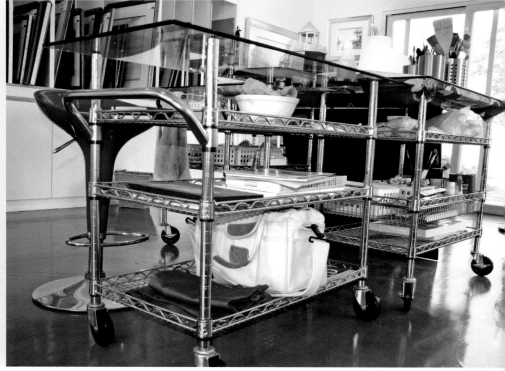

left: A separate area for watercolors and pastels keep supplies organized.

room, and studio areas. We decided it needed to be a functional space for teaching and display, as well as a working studio.

One day, before the money was really available to do the remodeling, we consulted with an architect. Enthusiastically, we shared the idea box and our large collection of scribbled notes. The architect wrote and sketched furiously.

A decision was made to collaborate on a creative design that would meet all of our requirements. Making it real mattered to us. Because it was so important and we could visualize the dream, we soon found the means to make it a reality.

We hired a contractor, and in a matter of several weeks, the dream was manifested. Sitting high on the hill, it resembled one of my light-washed paintings.

Inside, it contained all of our dream spaces: a painting studio for me and a stained-glass studio for my husband,

plus a teaching space and display area along with two offices and a guest suite.

The studio has an area for watercolors and an area for pastels. I keep the spaces separate because of the nature of the materials used. It also allows me to have a number of works going at the same time. Each area also has space for the supplies and materials needed to create the art. My husband has his spot for creating works of art with glass. When we designed the studio, we set up a space with a special splashguard for when he grinds glass. I also have an area dedicated to the dollhouse that I am building.

The watercolor area was designed using the top of our old kitchen table, which sits atop some movable carts with lots of space for supplies. The supplies are easy to see and reach. The entire center can be moved if teaching a class or cleaning the studio. This has helped to add flexibility to the space.

In order to protect the watercolor and pastel papers, shelving was designed and built that would hold full sheets of watercolor paper.

The studio also becomes the gallery from which art is shown and purchased.

The transformation has been amazing. The old, weather-beaten building for horses and tractors has become a magnificent, modern, light-filled space for reflection, contemplation, and creation. ✳

below: Part painting studio, part stained-glass studio, this creative space is used to teach, display, and sell art as well as being used as a working studio.

in her
SHOES

by **CATHERINE THURSBY**

ann arbor, michigan

INSIDE THE CREATIVE STUDIO

PHOTOS BY CATHERINE THURSBY

I have a small business and studio downtown called Red Shoes, where I sell art, vintage goods, children's things, and gifts. I chose to move my studio space downtown into my shop because I wanted to dedicate a larger, prettier space for myself that would inspire me to be more creative.

I felt that if my customers could come into the store and see what I was working on, it would be interesting for them to view the process and motivation for me to keep making and producing things more often.

12' (3.65 m)

desk with sewing machine		shelving
	table	shelving
sink		

12' (3.65 m)

CATHERINE'S STUDIO

Sweet glass jars hold many colorful treasures.

The one thing that I notice about most women/moms who are artists/crafters is how small a space we give ourselves. We usually only allow ourselves a tiny corner, a spot in the basement, or a closet, instead of a large dedicated space in which to create.

I was tired of always having my things put away, without easy access to create. I was also tired of having a mess on my kitchen table, which is where I mostly ended up anyway. So the decision to move my studio into a dedicated space at my shop was like a gift to myself. I deserved it!

During the first year downtown, I moved my studio downstairs into the shop basement during the holidays so we'd have more space for retail. But I found that I was basically doing the same thing that I had been doing at home, still not really allowing myself a truly dedicated space to create. When I finally realized that I needed to make my studio a number-one priority, my space really started to develop and become my little sanctuary.

My customers also really enjoyed taking a peek into how I worked. They enjoyed seeing my stacks of fabrics and jars of embellishments, my own personal collections of things. Those things inspired them, too.

Just having the larger windows and light, along with being able to see all of my supplies at hand, makes my creative juices start flowing. I love to use old cabinets and glass jars to house things such as pastels, old tiles, buttons, papers, and fabrics. My most favorite piece is a vintage display rack that was used to sell sandpaper in a hardware store; now it holds pretty scrapbooking papers! I love how the colors just pop against the rust.

My space is so full of light and pretty colors that it makes me feel good. And when you feel wonderful, you can create wonderful things.

I'm so happy I decided to put myself first for a change and really allow myself to have a place that I can truly call my own. It has definitely made a difference in the amount of work that I have been able to churn out. I have become more productive and more organized. And because my customers can see my creative space, I feel that I need to keep it fairly clean, so I am learning to work a little bit neater. That in itself is a miracle, because I tend to have explosive moments of creativity!

redshoeshomegoods.com

Wanting her customers to see what inspires her all day, Catherine moved her studio into her shop.

I still utilize parts of my basement to store larger items that take up too much floor space, such as bins that hold wool blankets and sweaters that I use for making my felted pillows. I also use that space for materials that are not so visually appealing. I try to keep the main area filled with the basic supplies of paint, papers, and small tools that I use on a daily basis.

My studio is a work in progress, a very dynamic space that I am still learning how to use effectively. But it has freed me from being a "transient" artist. I believe when you have a space that is yours entirely, it is truly freeing to the mind, which leads to more time being used to cultivate ideas instead of cleaning the kitchen table. To me, that is so worth it! ✳

CATHERINE'S SMALL SPACE TIPS:

1 Get a space of your own, even if it has to be small.

2 Make it personal to encourage your creativity.

3 Have a place off-site to keep bulky or seldom-used materials.

branching OUT

by MARGIE WOODS BROWN

dallas, texas

My studio is a dream come true for me. Being able to walk through my house and up the stairs into this magical space every day is the most amazing commute I could have ever dreamed up.

lotsaa.com

A closet turned wash station.
PHOTOS BY CHRIS WIEGAND

As I ascend, I leave the hustle and bustle of the world behind and enter a creative wonderland. The red linoleum floors invoke playful and imaginative energy, and the spacious, airy quality of the room inspires with its many possibilities. Art pieces—mine and those of loved ones—adorn the walls, and the shelves and tables that surround the room are packed with every necessary supply. If inspiration wanes, I simply look out one of the many windows and take in the beauty and power of the lovely Texas trees that frame the view. Sunlight fills the room all day, from every angle.

When I moved to Dallas from Venice, California, a year ago to be with my husband, we had a vision of finding a home with studio spaces for both of us (he is a musician). Even though our real estate agent thought we were delusional, we held to our dream. This was the first house we looked at, and we scooped it up. After a major renovation, we have both settled in and are running our businesses from home.

Although my studio space was close to perfect to begin with, it was fun to customize it to meet my needs. I kept it very simple and open, as that was one of the things I loved about it when I first walked in. I designed

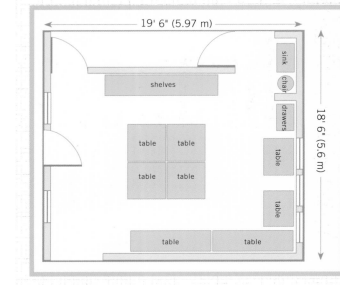

MARGIE'S STUDIO

Built-in shelves hold anything and everything.

a huge wall of built-in square shelves that hold everything from books to art supplies. I also had a closet converted to a wash station, complete with a huge laundry sink. I am thrilled not to have to use bathroom sinks anymore for washing my brushes! My favorite items in the studio are the four custom-made moveable tables. They are 3' × 4' with glass tops for easy clean up. They stand 3' high, so it is easy to work while standing or to use a stool.

I love the versatility of my tables: I can separate them for a workshop of up to eight people or bring them all together to create a huge work space for myself. As I've broken-in my space, paint patterns have built up on the tables and spills adorn the floors. I love this evolution, as it builds character and reminds me of all of the creative souls with whom I have shared this space. My office and life-coaching areas are adjacent to the studio, so I'm able to do all aspects of my work in this one cohesive, creative space that sits up in the treetops above our home.

My absolute favorite thing about it all is that at the end of the day I can walk down the stairs and be with my family. I am so very grateful! ☀

NO ROOM TO BE CREATIVE?

Not so! Consider these alternatives:

- Landing at the top of the stairs
- Nook under the stairs
- Attic
- Room over the garage
- Garage loft
- Desk in the kitchen or mudroom
- Closet
- Seldom-used formal dining room
- Tray table
- Corner of bedroom
- Armoire
- Wheeled cart and desktop
- Kids' playhouse
- Shed
- Balcony
- Porch

Red linoleum floors spark energy and creativity in Margie's airy studio space.

hay loft
TO ARTIST'S LOFT

by **SARA LECHNER**

mank, austria

My studio is a long-wished-for dream come true. I live on a farm near the Alps in Austria (the wine country and Danube are just a few miles away), with a big family (nine in all) plus hens and sheep.

PHOTOS BY PABLO JÄGER

I never had enough space to work in the building, and after moving my art supplies from one room to the other, always looking for better storage space, light, and enough isolation from the human and zoological multitudes to concentrate, my husband and I decided to convert the floor that formerly held hay and straw into a studio.

Because it had to cost nothing (or next to nothing), we used our own straw bales and adobe mud to insulate the wood walls and did all the work ourselves. It took about three years to finish the construction. Sensing that my husband was skeptical about how I would use all 4,000 square feet, I decided to add a small open kitchen and a coffee corner so I could offer workshops to fill the place. I needn't have worried. At

least one-fifth of the space was soon filled with loads of materials. For sorting them, I bought about seventy-five bookshelves for a very fair price and got all my things organized for the first time in my life. I found materials I never knew I had during this endeavor! Because I work with textiles, paper, metal, wool, paints, and mixed media, I really needed those seventy-five bookshelves. The shelves are separated in families of materials, colors, qualities, and frequency of use. The extra-big items such as fabric bolts, batting, paper rolls, and cushion fillings have their own, separate spaces.

I used plastic boxes to store the small materials and tools. I labeled the boxes alphabetically and sorted the small things I am always looking for but that are difficult to organize—such as tweezers or shrink plastic—in

thefabricofmeditation.blogspot.com

these boxes. Of course, if you're like me and have a family where you speak two or more languages, you will appreciate the problem I had—never knowing which language to use for labeling things. This adds to the sport!

The rest of the space is separated into other areas without walls, but with some variation in the height of the floor. There is the coffee room; the gallery of works from my Web friends; the exhibition of my works; a country art corner; a place for two huge, very old looms ripe for a museum (I do not weave, but a friend was looking for a place where she could store them, and I thought it could be a nice addition to the ambience); the "wet" studio to work with paints, felting, and water techniques; and the "dry" studio with sewing and felting machines and worktables. In the middle of the studio are the wood stoves; I am building glass walls that will surround the stoves and a small work area so that I have a heated place to work in during the winter. It was too energy-intensive to heat the whole building during the cold season.

Another issue was the lighting—you lose a lot of light in such an open space. To solve this problem, I installed different kinds of lighting: overhead lights for an all-around effect and fluorescent light tubes with "daylight" over the tables to accurately see the colors I'm working with. There is also a more cozy setting for the after-work activities. I installed several power outlets around the room, as well: you can never have too much light or too many electric sockets.

I never would have dreamed of having a studio this expansive if we hadn't already had the raw space and building materials on the farm. An added bonus is that I have to walk miles inside it collecting the material I need for my work. Before I had my studio, I exercised very little and sat at the computer or sewed and stitched most of the day. Now I'm always fit for a mountain hike! ✷

left: A friend's vintage loom adds to the ambience.

right: The entrance to Sara's studio.

below: Sara's seventy-five bookshelves hold all her materials.

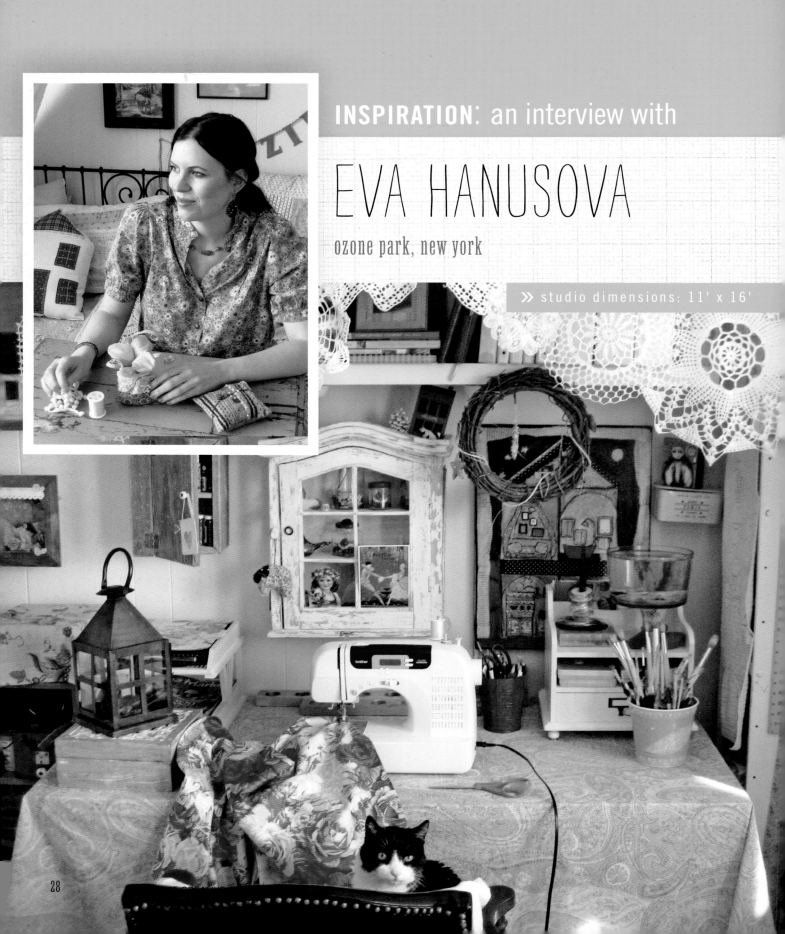

INSPIRATION: an interview with

EVA HANUSOVA

ozone park, new york

» studio dimensions: 11' x 16'

evahanusova.com

what I do: Mixed-media painting

why my space works for me: A great part of my art celebrates the beauty of nature, whimsy, and romance. I am constantly amazed by the sketches nature draws each day, inspiring me to capture the beauty of it in my own way.

I am a lucky girl to have a space of my own that I can call my enchanting sanctuary. Anytime I feel little down and blue, this is the place to be and get my energy up. The space is very calming with a homey atmosphere, and no matter where I look, each object evokes only positive feelings within me, and the stories and creative spirit flow. Since I have a passion for old found objects as well as hues of turquoise and green, this is reflected in my style and surroundings. These things cast a magic spell over me, and I always try to incorporate them in everything I do.

My studio is not very spacious, but I make it work for me and my art by moving objects around to keep things fresh and unique. I try to de-clutter once in a while, but as I am a collector of all things beautiful, this is a constant challenge for me. I am a big fan of artfully arranged displays, from supplies and materials to inspirational images or collections, and believe that anything has the possibility to become useful and functional storage. I have been using tea-light candle holders to store stones and beads for my jewelry, jars for bits and pieces of ribbons, baskets for my fabric and yarn, and bowls and wooden cabinets for my glitter, which I leave open when I work to stimulate the creative energy and keep the ideas flowing.

Everything in my studio has a story of its own that enhances the atmosphere of the space. ✳

MY FAVORITE THINGS

The wrought-iron bed. It elevates my studio from being simply a working space to the perfect lounging spot for my family and friends, and it allows me to dream in between my projects. I think my cat spends more time on the bed than anybody else, but when the time is right, it is the best place to crash.

chapter 2

ORGANIZATION AND STORAGE

"When it comes to organizing,
we all have our preferences.
Some people love everything
in its place and hidden away.
I, however, am a digger."

—TIM HOLTZ

Artists seem to fall into two categories: the ones who like all their materials in plain sight and the ones who like to work with clear decks and a clean slate. The former tend to enjoy the unexpected discoveries that come from a jumble of colors, textures, and media. The latter find freedom in knowing they can lay their hands on the particular paint tube or fabric square they need the moment inspiration strikes.

Regardless of which end of the spectrum you lean toward, at some point you will find that you have too much stuff. You can't find that favorite stamp you know you just saw somewhere or your supplies no longer fit in your neatly labeled bins. That's when you have to purge, sort, and delete. And that can be hard.

But the artists in this chapter have it figured out, and they're eager to share how they organize, store, de-stash, and do it all creatively.

CLUTTER OUT, CREATIVITY IN

10 STEPS to a more artful studio
by **LESLEY RILEY**

fabric creep (verb) fab•rik krēp

1. The slow, steady migration of a fabric stash beyond the boundaries of its designated storage containers

2. A condition created when fabric covertly overtakes your surroundings

3. A situation created by uncontrolled fabric acquisition and hoarding

Fabric Creep is the term my husband (lovingly?) gave to the bins and piles of fabric that were overtaking our bedroom, aka my studio. He was very understanding and just grateful that I had left him a path to his closet. Perhaps some of you are in a similar situation and have already diagnosed yourself with fabric creep. I'm going to help you combat it in a way that not only clears out the clutter, but makes you more creative. Please feel free to apply these methods to buttons, found papers, rubber stamps, books, and anything else you hoard.

Last spring, before I even knew I was going to be moving and downsizing, I realized I had to come to terms with this situation and bring it under control. Fortunately, I was artistically mature enough to realize that I no longer needed all of this fabric. By artistically mature, I mean that over the years I have come to know myself as an artist—the fabrics I favor; the colors, patterns, and textures I turn to over and over again. I decided to divide my fabrics into three categories:

1 **My favorites**

2 **The ones I use on a regular basis, but not my favorites**

3 **The ones I know I'll never use but, hey, it's fabric, and I might need it someday**

And did I mention that there was not only fabric in the bedroom, but in the upstairs hallway and in the basement? Fabric is to a quilter what paint is to a painter. Because you cannot mix fabrics the way you can mix paint, you need a larger palette of colors/designs/ textures to choose from. Plus, I really use my fabric and sell much of what I make with it, so acquiring it had been a necessity and a business expense. At least, that's what I told myself for many years. But that much? Really!

When the time came to downsize the stash, I knew exactly what to do. Knowing how exciting it is to acquire fabric, especially from another artist, I thought I'd share the wealth. For ten bucks plus Priority Mail shipping, you could get a USPS flat-rate box of (color-coordinated!) scraps from my stash. And I do mean

FIVE WAYS TO MAKE
PARTING EASIER

1 WORK WITH A BUDDY. A friend who supports your downsizing efforts will help keep you going and keep you from losing perspective. With any luck, she'll take stuff home with her.

2 DO A LITTLE AT A TIME. Downsizing your entire stash in one sitting is not only impossible, it's overwhelming. So don't. Set aside enough time to go through one drawer or one shelf. Have a box or bin handy for the discards. Then make an appointment with yourself to do the next drawer or shelf.

3 GO DIGITAL. Scan found papers, photos, vintage wallpaper, even fabrics (for their pattern) and sell or give away the originals. Megabytes take up much less space than objects.

4 GOT A FABRIC WHOSE PATTERN YOU JUST LOVE, BUT DOESN'T FIT IN WITH YOUR ART MAKING? Treat it as art in and of itself. Frame a piece of it and sell or give away the rest. Same goes for buttons and rubber stamps: frame or display your favorites and downsize the remainder.

5 NO GUILT, NO REGRETS Okay, so you never finished the batik and macramé project you started in college or used the silk fabric in colors you hate that your sister-in-law brought you from her trip to Thailand. Get over it. Either recycle the materials into a new project or give them away. Nobody's keeping score.

lesleyriley.com

scraps. I had already donated all the yardage I had to a local senior center.

So then came the hard part: deciding what stayed and what went. Of course all the Category 1 fabric would stay and all the Category 3 could go, but the bulk of my stash fell into Category 2, and that's where it got hard. Along the way, I learned a few things. If you, too, need to take control of or eradicate fabric creep, here are the methods I used, the realizations I gained, and the lessons I learned. ➤➤

1 HOARDING IS A PRIMITIVE INSTINCT. **But it is not necessary for your survival as a fabric artist. In fact, having a limited selection of fabrics forces you to be more creative and make better design decisions. You learn to alter the fabric that's available or even to create your own by dyeing or painting or surface design.**

2 KNOW THYSELF. **If you're like me, you have been collecting fabric since forever. But over the years I developed preferences and a style that made use of only a small portion of my stash. I realized that I had outgrown or moved beyond most of my fabrics. Think about which fabric/colors/patterns/textures, etc., you turn to again and again. Keep those and get rid of the others.**

3 TREAT YOUR STASH LIKE YOUR CLOTHES. **The rule is, if you haven't worn it in a year, get rid of it. Be honest with yourself as you review each piece of fabric. Have you used any of it in the last year or two? If not, pass it on.**

4 IT'S NOT ALL OR NOTHING. **Don't be hard on yourself. It's your stash, you don't have to get rid of everything, and you don't have to whittle it down in one sitting. You can do it over time, especially if you know you'll have a hard time parting with any of it. What's a "must keep" in the spring might become a giveaway by fall.**

5 TAKE YOUR TIME. **Moving to a new home or just into a new studio space is the perfect time to review your stash. But if that's not in your plan, just set a reasonable deadline and work on it a little at a time. At first, like me, you might hold back a lot of fabric. But once you start sorting, you will probably discover that parting with it becomes easier.**

6 SHARE FAVORITES. **One of the best parts of the downsizing process was sharing my favorites. When I teach, I often take snippets of my favorite fabrics to share with the class. Often, it's the addition of one of my fabrics that makes their piece sing. Downsize your good stuff by cutting off a fat eighth or quarter to share at your next group activity.**

7 SPREAD THE WEALTH. **There are many organizations that would love to have your excess fabric. Larger pieces can go to a senior center or any charity organization that has quilting or sewing classes. And don't forget your local schools, camps, theaters. Anything from snippets to cuttings to fat quarters can find a home in a student's art project. And obviously, if you take a bag full of fabric to your local quilt guild, it will disappear before you can finish saying "giveaway."**

8 CREATE COORDINATED BUNDLES. **Because of my large stash, I was able to create theme bundles: fabric with writing, kitschy and kitchen bundles, vintage bundles—you get the idea. These bundles are great to sell on Etsy, through your blog, or at a show or guild sale. Many people who are new to fabric arts or quilting don't have the time, money, or know-how to assemble a set of coordinating fabrics for specific projects or classes, and these bundles suit their needs perfectly.**

9 THE ARTIST, NOT THE FABRIC, MAKES THE ART. **Fabric can become a crutch you fall back on instead of moving into the scary unknown called art making. A perceived lack of fabric or "just the right fabric" is really just an excuse not to create. You don't need more fabric—you need to use what you have.**

10 YOU CONTROL THE FABRIC. **The fabric does not control you. Fabric creep occurs when you let the fabric take over and control your life and surroundings. I understand, I truly do— it's pretty, you like to see and caress it, and just knowing it's there makes you feel secure. It's your lifeblood and the tool of your creativity. I know you love it, but sometimes when you love something you must let it go.** ✳

disarray
TO DISPLAY

by GINA LEE KIM

salisbury, massachusetts

The awful truth: I was living in excess and monster clutter. I had way too much stuff, and I felt guilty about it. So I told myself that every single thing I currently possessed had to have a home in my new space, otherwise it was tossed, recycled, sold, or given away. My vision was to combine order and beauty. Here's how I did it.

GINA'S TIPS AND HINTS:

1 Organize ribbons by threading a dowel suspended beneath a shelf.

2 Turn a garden trellis into an idea board with S-hooks.

3 Leave unfinished work out of the way on a freestanding shelf.

PHOTOS BY JIM HULLY

I ordered a black craft table online and bought two stools so that if a friend is visiting, we can craft across from each other. I also love how this table stores all my art books on one side and hides all my acrylic paints and my heat gun on the other side.

My craft storage center (or as my husband calls it "Gina's Craft Store") also serves as a writing area. When I'm not crafting, I open the glass doors. It brings such creative delight—it's cheerful even to sit and pay my bills! The desk and hutch and two narrow side book-shelves give great vertical storage for a small space.

The middle shelf of one bookcase holds my rubber stamp collection, paper punches, and adhesives. If I cannot see something or it's buried in cluttered layers, that means I'm probably not using it or have too much of it, and I eventually give it away. That's the value of organizing—to see what you have in excess.

To keep my ribbons in order, I got an inexpensive wooden dowel rod from the hardware store and suspend-ed it from beneath the bottom shelf inside my hutch. It's anchored with wires and safe adhesives to protect the furniture's surface.

I'm constantly rearranging my idea area, with a three-foot freestanding black shelf I purchased at a fur-niture store. This is where I "rest" my unfinished paint-ings. It also holds some of my frequently used acrylic gel mediums.

I often buy cards as mini-artworks and clip pictures out of magazines for color inspiration. My clothesline where I display them is a ¼" wide ribbon suspended tightly with hooks (two on each end and one in the center).

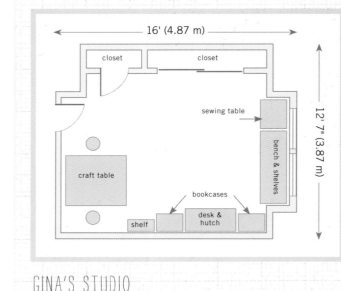

GINA'S STUDIO

ginaleekim.com

Instead of building a customized window seat, I bought a cushioned bench on sale and put it directly under the window. I removed the cheap baskets that came with the bench and turned the unit into a bookshelf/seating area to hold my large coffee table books.

I used suction cups that come with S-hooks to hang some of my square mixed-media collage paintings. A trifold mirror purchased from an outlet is my "wall" that also reflects light. My studio does not have a lot of wall space, so this is my mini-gallery, for now.

I keep all my tubes of gouache and watercolors in my second closet, where I also store large-sized frames. I bought a pretty organizer box from a discount store that neatly and conveniently holds all my colored tissue papers (and it fits perfectly into my bookshelf when not in use). Adding a large rubber band makes retrieving tissues quick and easy without everything spilling out.

Today, this former spare bedroom/extra storage area is something that I can proudly call my own—a creative retreat within our condo. It may have been time-consuming to pull together all the furnishings, but it was worth it to be able to display the things I treasure in a functional way, as beautifully as I can. I love it in here. It's not always tidy, but with creative use of furniture and my own DIY storage solutions, I'm able to put things back in order when I want to. ✺

left: Gina's craft storage center. Inset, lower left.

top left: top left: A bench bought on sale acts as a makeshift window seat.

top right: I needed a huge idea board. I chose three garden trellises I bought on sale and mounted them side by side with strategically placed S-hooks hung on them. Now I have the liberty to hang my artwork (finished/unfinished), color inspiration, notes, and so on.

left: Unfinished paintings rest on a store-bought black shelf.

made
TO ORDER

by **JANE DÁVILA**

ridgefield, connecticut

When my husband, an oil painter of very large abstracts, and I were looking for a house seven years ago, we had a specific list of requirements, and a separate studio space for each of us was at the top of the list.

THINGS WORTH HAVING

1 Flowerpots to hold tools and supplies

2 A media cart to hold magazines and books

3 Curtain panels that hang in front of fabric shelves
to prevent fading

Our current house suits us very well: his studio is the 20' × 24' barn on our property; my studio is the attached sunroom off the living room in the main house.

There are advantages and drawbacks to a sunroom as a studio. The light is amazing, but it can also cause problems. There are windows on three walls of the room and the fourth wall has a set of side-lighted French doors leading to the living room. This means there is almost no wall space. And no closet. Storage, therefore, is the biggest issue, and I've had to be very creative. I built most of the furniture in the room myself so I could make it fit the space exactly and provide the storage and functionality I need at the right height for me.

I made a large rolling island using my parents' old kitchen butcher-block tabletop as the starting point, adding shelves for storage on three sides. The short side holds flowerpots, a favorite storage device of mine (they're pretty, waterproof, and portable), for a wide variety of small things such as stamp pads, pastels, gouache, paint daubers, small found objects for printing, Bazzill chips, and other tools and raw materials. I love the principle of repetition and apply it to my studio as well as my art. Visual clutter is very distracting to me, and I find it hard to create in this kind of overstimulation. Repeating shapes and colors in the elements of my studio keeps the visual chaos to a minimum. Because my studio is visible from the living room and is in public space, I like it to look clean and inviting and more finished than a typical studio might. I find it to be a very inspirational space to work in, and I'm close to the action.

janedavila.com

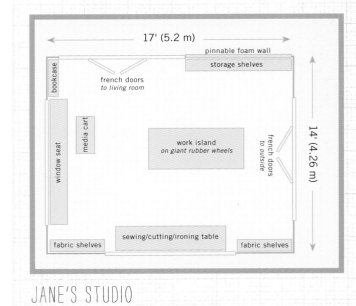

JANE'S STUDIO

ESSENTIAL ELEMENTS

Whether you set up a creative space in a closet or a corner of your basement or you have the luxury of a dedicated studio space in your home or at another location, there are a few essential elements that most everyone needs:

- A surface where you can spread out your work (fabric, mixed media, paint, etc.), set at a height that makes it comfortable for you to sit or stand (given your preference)

- Clear or labeled storage so you can find what you need quickly

- A place to set items that are finished or in progress

- An inspiration spot—this could be a pin-up board, a window seat, artwork, etc.

I built a window seat by starting with two flat files from Dick Blick to anchor each end of the unit. I store my finished art quilts (I work small!) and art papers in these drawers. I divided the space between the flat files into thirds and added doors. In these cubbies, I keep my thread collection in plastic storage boxes (arranged by type and color), more paper, and a backup sewing machine.

My 8' sewing/cutting/ironing table is the height of a kitchen countertop. My husband built this unit when we lived in a previous house, but it fits nicely in this one.

It has a lot of storage space below, and the large flat drawers are wonderful for storing rulers, mats, and large pads of paper.

More flowerpots in my studio hold paintbrushes of every size, marking tools and scissors, inks, paint sticks and colored pencils, paints, and printing supplies.

Below my design wall is a unit I constructed specifically to hold white metal bins with all of my surface-design supplies and materials. Small bins hold glitter, Angelina fibers, Pearl Ex powders, stamp-carving tools and blocks, beads, and wire. Silk, wool, fiber postcard

above: Spice jars with magnetic bases hold stamps and embellishments on metal strips attached to the wall. Repetition of containers creates a sense of uniformity.

supplies, found objects, yarns and trims, glues, adhesives, and fixatives are in large bins.

I also built a media cart to house my collection of magazines; recent acquisitions are in three pockets on one side, held in with a custom-cut and -drilled piece of acrylic.

I have found that kitchen organizers are very handy in the studio. They're meant to contain and hold at the ready an assortment of small things in an attractive manner. I use spice jars with magnetic bases to hold stamps and embellishments on metal strips attached to the wall. A drawer organizer holds small bottles of paint and tools, and racks mounted to the inside of cabinet doors hold gel media and glues.

My fabric stash lives on two large shelf units, neatly stacked and organized by color. To prevent fading, I made curtain panels to hang over the fabric, hung from tension rods fitted to the inside of the top shelves. I can easily remove the curtain panel when I need to access my fabric and replace it when I'm done. I would eventually like to replace these fabric panels with doors with frosted acrylic inserts.

Lighting is not a problem during the day—not with windows on three sides and four skylights overhead—but at night it can be problematic. I installed three sets of

track lights on each of the three overhead beams. Halogen lighting keeps the room bright and fairly evenly lit.

Two houses ago, my studio consisted of a closet with bifold doors in the living room. We built in shelves and a countertop to hold my machine. It was literally only 6' wide and 18" deep. In our last house, I took over the 7' × 9' den, with no closet, and thought I was in heaven—a room of my own! I love my current studio and love creating in it. And at 16 square feet, it'll be a while before I outgrow it. ✳

above: Flowerpots in all shapes and sizes hold paints, pencils, inks, tools, and printing supplies.

holtz
everything

by **TIM HOLTZ**

prescott, arizona

For me, being surrounded by the things that inspire me is key to my creativity. Now, I know; not everyone has the space to create their ultimate craft haven, but honestly, it doesn't take much. People are often surprised when they enter my studio and see that it's not a fancy add-on. Located right off of the kitchen, my studio was once the master bedroom in my four-bedroom home.

INSIDE THE CREATIVE STUDIO

timholtz.com

For many years, I had worked in very close quarters. But priorities finally took over and the move was on. While I was on a teaching trip, two of my close friends decided it was time to make the switch. Seriously, it was like one of those TV shows where amazing transformations happen in your home while you're away. I came home to find my supplies—once tucked away in plastic cart drawers and closet shelves—now visible and spread out. Because my friends had already done the moving part, I took over the organizing of supplies. A little tweaking of furniture here and there, and my very own studio came to life.

When it comes to organizing, we all have our preferences. Some people love drawers, compartments, and dividers—everything in its place and hidden away. I, however, am a digger. I think that creativity often stems from seeing the ordinary through different eyes, and most of the time when I'm looking for a particular

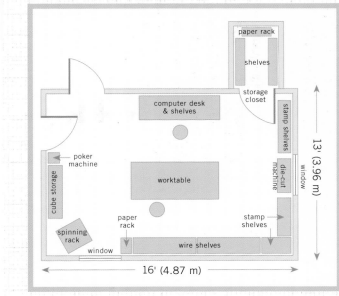

TIM'S STUDIO

object, I come across the unexpected. This works for me: having everything out in the open so I can see it, dig through it, and most importantly, use it!

I admit I am a collector of sorts, I like ephemera, all things vintage, found objects, the trash-to-treasure kinds of finds, and, oh yeah—inks, paints, stamps, and any craft tool I can discover. So obviously, having everything in its place and a place for everything is often a challenge in itself. But I believe in organized chaos. I've found a few things that work for me that I want to share with you. Let's explore my creative world a little and hopefully you'll find at least one idea to bring you one step closer to creating the studio of your dreams.

As you enter the studio, you'll see that everything revolves around my center craft table. This sturdy block table was once the dining room table. I like real-furniture tables because they provide a sturdier surface than folding worktables. All of my other supplies surround the table. I like this floor plan because I can work my way around the room freely and see everything from one spot.

The units directly behind my table hold the most frequently used supplies, tools, trims, and objects. These restaurant-style units can hold up to 650 pounds per shelf! That means I don't have to worry about overloading anything, and I like that. I purchased several wire drawers, baskets, and bins from local discount

stores. Having everything in wire storage allows me to see what's where and even more importantly, gives me easy access to it all. On the top of the unit, I inserted a curtain rod through my ribbon spools and hung it from the top shelf with S-hooks. This way, I was able to thread my ribbons through the wavy portion of the wire rack, and it works perfectly. The most random part of this space is the top shelf where all the good stuff is kept. I started collecting vintage locker baskets to house my findings and antique wares. The baskets are eclectic and sturdy enough for me to load them up with my trinkets and sift through them, too.

Next to the table stands the heart and soul of my studio: my tools of the trade. The spinner rack is by far my most treasured fixture. I picked it up from my old job at a craft store where the owner was actually throwing it out! It's a four-sided wood unit with adjustable shelving, on a spinning base. It's perfect in every way: it holds every ink pad, paint dabber, embossing powder, crackle paint, re-inker, and any bottles I can't find a place for. Organization at its finest.

On one of the outer walls, I have bookcases from floor to ceiling. This room has a vaulted ceiling, so the shelves go from 6' on one end of the wall to 12' on the other, and they are packed. I display all my rubber stamps on these shelves at an angle so I can fit more and see a little of each image. I made risers in the back

of each shelf so I can also store the stamps two layers deep. The risers are made of foam insulation from the hardware store—again simple and affordable. If you're a stamper, then like me you often buy stamps just because they look cool, whether you use them or not. For this reason, each unit is lit from above to showcase the stamps.

The closet in this former master bedroom didn't go to waste, either. The shelves and rods were removed and replaced with four more of the industrial restaurant shelves. Here, I store and organize all of my craft supplies for workshops and kits, including extra inks, paints, and paper. I have every bin labeled, but again, those are just guidelines. Remember, I'm a digger, so most of these bins are just generally categorized odds and ends. Is this a vault full of crafting goodness or what?

Just outside the closet is a cabinet unit that holds a computer, a couple of printers, books, and catalogs. This is where the business stuff is handled—it can't all be fun and game.

As you look around the rest of my studio, you'll find that just about every space is packed full of random and eclectic objects, from suitcases, locks, keys, printer's blocks, hands, and doll heads to a cymbal-playing monkey—most people think he's creepy, but I love him! I also created a hanging art piece from my very first signature product, Distress Inks, and hung each stamp pad case right on the wall. There's even a real working poker machine in the studio for the occasional, but much-needed, breaks from being creative.

This is what inspires me. You may have different ideas. But wherever your artistic and creative journey takes you, I recommend you find your own creative space—big or small. The most important thing is to make it work for you, make it inspire you, and live the life you've imagined. ✳

above: A former closet in the master bedroom now houses papers, paints, inks, and more.

FITS TO a T

by **RENAY LEONE**

excelsior, minnesota

The bonus room over our two-and-a-half car garage was left unfinished when we built our house ten years ago. After a few years, my husband conceded that its highest and best use would be as a studio for my fiber art work (his model railroad layout takes up most of the basement).

The room is T-shaped and is in the northeast corner of the house, so natural light is plentiful but not too hot or damaging to fibers. With a backdrop of white and black, windows on three sides and plenty of additional track lighting, plus most furniture on wheels, this adaptable space lets me go anywhere I want—color-wise, fiber-wise, and time-wise—with the ability to leave big messes for later inspiration and eventual cleanup.

My favorite quote, "Use the talents you possess, for the woods would be silent if no birds sang except the best" by Henry Van Dyke, is stenciled on the wall over my fabric storage area. It helps keep me grounded, yet lets me fly in new fiber directions and reminds me of the

PHOTOS BY GERRY LEONE

RENAY'S TIPS & HINTS:

1 Square floor tiles offer a flat surface and reliable grid for squaring up and basting quilts in process.

2 Knee walls provide a perfect space for roll-out fabric storage.

3 Tables outfitted with wheeled bases make them a more comfortable height to work at while standing.

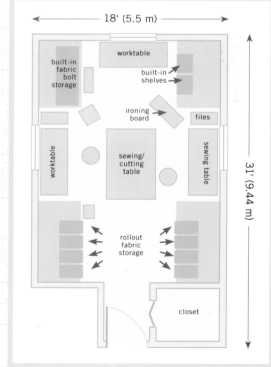

RENAY'S STUDIO

be silent if no birds sang except for the best.

need we all have to be who we are, no matter what our work lives may be. (I'm a recovering attorney.)

My favorite storage idea came from the five-foot-high knee walls on either side of the room. We were able to fit roll-out stacking wire baskets storage for all my fabric stash in between the studs, making the fabric both accessible and easy to put away. Other great features include long rolled storage (behind another knee wall on the far side of the room) for completed quilts; cubbies in the walls for CDs, magazines, quilting and knitting books; shelves over the door for jars that hold my button collection; and a type case and clear lamp base for my wooden spool collection. Storage for threads and beads are simple hardware-store containers. Using fifteen dollars' worth of supplies from a big-box retailer, my husband made a 5' × 2' cover for the standard ironing board top. This is great for ironing yards of fabric, and the top comes off if I need the tapered end for actual clothes ironing (not very often).

renayleone@earthlink.net

above: The built-in long cabinet stores finished quilts.

The tables for the cutting/sewing workspace in the center of the room were purchased secondhand at an office-supply warehouse. We attached them to each other and then mounted them on wheeled bases made by my husband, for a more comfortable height when I'm standing. Everything is detachable so the tables can be rearranged. A third table of the same kind is set against the far (design) wall and is also on wheels. The design wall is made of Styrofoam and used for auditioning fabrics or photographing completed works. The window provides a lovely view of my garden when the wall is not in use. The black and white square vinyl tiles on the floor are easy to keep clean, make it easy to find lost pins, and provide a flat surface and reliable grid for squaring up and basting quilts in process.

Yarn storage is mostly in wire bins and on a store display tower/plant rack at the back of the room. Miscellaneous fibers and embellishments are in shoe boxes and more roll-out shelving in the closet, making it all available and accessible and a bit less messy to look at all the time.

Our cat, Phyllis, is my studio assistant. She loves to explore most projects in process as well as after completion—if she gets a chance. ✺

101 ORGANIZATION AND STORAGE TIPS

Holly Berube made this craft area with two storage closets from IKEA, some simple shelving, and added a designer touch with fabric on the doors.

When we have asked readers what they most wanted to see in *Studios*, the #1 choice—by far—is always "organization and storage tips." So, here are 101 of our favorite organization and storage tips for your studio, big or small, fabulous or frugal.

CORSETED CANS BY MEGAN LAPP

7 all-time great
ORGANIZATION TIPS

KNOW YOUR ORGANIZATIONAL STYLE. Maybe you toss all your colored pencils and marking pens into the same bin at the end of the day. Maybe you can't sleep unless each pencil is arranged by color in descending order and safely snapped into its slot in the original case. The way and the degree to which you organize is up to you, so don't fight your natural style. Go with it.

CREATE ZONES. If your space is big enough, make a zone for each kind of task, e.g., a sewing area, a cutting and pressing area, a wet area, and a sketching area. Or a paper area and a bead area. Keep all your supplies for that task in that zone. If this means buying two pairs of needle-nose pliers, one for your handstitching zone and one for your beading area, so be it.

COLOR COORDINATE. Whether you organize all your books by color or choose one color of bins for all sewing materials and another color for your beading stash, color can help you find what you're looking for faster.

MOVE IT OR LOSE IT. Don't have enough room to create zones? Use lightweight portable baskets or canvas bins to move supplies from shelf to table (and back). Also, put tables and drawers on wheels for more flexibility.

HAVE A PLACE TO KEEP YOUR STUFF. Whether it's a compartmentalized caddy or a tin can labeled "scissors" doesn't matter. What matters is not having to spend valuable creating time searching for the pinking shears you know are around here . . . somewhere.

PUT IT BACK. Once you have a place for your stuff, put it there when you're done. Do you ever lose your toothbrush when you're at home? No, because you always put it back in the same place every time you use it.

SCHEDULE TIME TO CLEAN UP. Always leave five to fifteen minutes for basic tidying: putting tools away, dumping paint water, tossing rubbish. A major clean-up isn't necessary. Just do whatever it takes to make it easy for you to begin again the next time.

MELANIE TESTA'S STUDIO. PHOTO BY MELANIE TESTA

5 inexpensive STORAGE TECHNIQUES

CARDBOARD COVER-UP. **Cover shoe boxes or copy-paper boxes with contact or wrapping paper for pretty, functional storage.**

HANG 'EM HIGH. **A clothesline or metal "zipline" attached near the top of the wall is a great place to keep finished or in-progress art or inspiration pieces.**

COUNTER INTELLIGENCE. **If you have a counter, or even a long table or desk, you probably have space below it that is going to waste. This is a great place to keep stacked bins or rolling drawers or shelving. Add doors or a skirt, and your storage is out of sight.**

FIND YOUR NICHE. **Make use of that funny jog in the wall, the exposed studs in an attic room, or a tiny closet by installing a cupboard or shallow shelves.**

TRAY CHIC. **Keep projects in process on trays that you can stack or slide onto a shelf until you're ready for them again.**

MARY CARLSON'S STUDIO. PHOTO BY RON AYOTTE AND MARIANNE LASSITER

MARCHEN STUDIOS. PHOTO BY LEAH VIS

2 INSTANT (almost) craft stations

1 Instant Craft Station #1: Make a craft area with inexpensive DIY freestanding closets, pegboard, and basic shelving units.

2 Instant Craft Station #2: Turn an unused computer armoire into a sewing or crafting station.

- Store your sewing machine on the desk shelf or slide it into the space for the computer processing unit when the doors are closed; sit it on the pull-out shelf to sew.

- If there isn't already a shelf on top, install one and/or a removable rod on which to slide ribbon rolls.

- Apply cork to the insides of the doors where you can pin inspirations photos, patterns, etc.

- Top the unit with a thrifted, painted hutch for more storage.

7 ways to make A DOOR work for you

- Over-the-door shelving racks are great for keeping your supplies in order.

- Clear shoe bags that hook onto the door are perfect for stashing yarns or rubber stamps.

- Tack ribbon to the door in a crisscross pattern to make a bulletin board that holds cards, papers, and swatches for inspiration.

- A door makes a great ironing station. There are racks made to hold a fold-down ironing board and the iron as well.

- Make a worktable or cutting area out of a hollow-core door placed on top of two sets of drawers.

- Turn a door into a pressing table by covering it with batting and muslin.

- Put it on the entrance to your studio and close it when you leave the room. Bye-bye, mess!

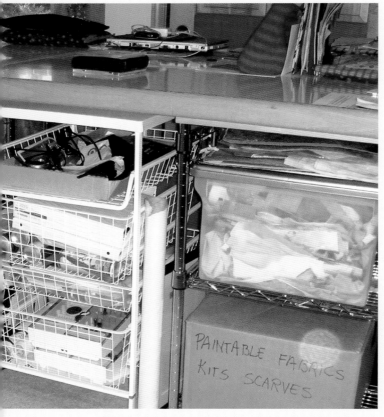

YVONNE PORCELLA'S STUDIO. PHOTO BY YVONNE PORCELLA

JENNIFER STEPANSKI'S STUDIO.
PHOTO BY JENNIFER STEPANSKI

3 ways to get ON BOARD

- PEGBOARD. Paint it a bright color to inspire you and keep it from looking like your dad's garage.
- HOMOSOTE. Cover it with plain flannel or muslin to make a design board.
- FOAM CORE. Covered with flannel, makes a lightweight, portable design wall.

5 ways to keep fibers, ribbons, and floss from TANGLING

- Hang on large key rings.
- Thread rolls onto dowels.
- Stack rolls onto vertical paper-towel holders.
- Wind onto craft sticks or clothespins and place in a jar or bowl.
- Grasp them with metal clips and hang clips on pegs or hooks on the wall.

4 uses for old GYM BASKETS (or new wire baskets)

- Fat quarters
- Large found objects
- Dyed wool fibers
- Felted wool

5 CONTAINERS for holding writing implements, paintbrushes, scissors, and small tools

- Cans
- Flowerpots
- Pails
- Silverware dividers
- Pressed-glass bud vases

KASS HALL'S STUDIO. PHOTO BY J. G. HALL

16 best VINTAGE ITEMS for storage

1 Old goblet trophies (for pens, paintbrushes)

2 Tiered or footed candy dishes (perfect for jewelry, found objects, rolled ribbons)

3 Toast racks (to organize cards, small notebooks)

4 Funky 1950s and 1960s ashtrays (great for buttons, beads, pins)

5 Enamel bowls and pans (great for stacking fabrics or holding paints)

6 Salt and pepper shakers (for sprinkling glitter)

7 Cigar boxes (for just about anything)

8 Wooden toolboxes (for paint and ink bottles)

9 Sewing table drawers (patterns, threads)

10 Mason jars (buttons, ribbons, paintbrushes)

11 Vintage locker bins for fat quarters by color/hue

12 Jars in every shape and size (from pasta sauce, pickles, capers, you name it) can store all kinds of things in them (buttons, bits of ribbon, yarn, thread, even fabric scraps in the big ones).

13 Plastic ice cube trays are just deep enough to hold brayers, wire tools, bookbinding tools, and other sets of supplies that need a home in the studio.

14 A BobbinSaver bobbin holder. It's a bagel-shaped piece that holds metal or plastic bobbins snugly so they won't unwind or tangle.

15 Fixtures from stores that have closed, such as spinning racks for books and DVDs.

16 Old lunch boxes come in handy for stamps, ribbons, and lace.

BETZ WHITE'S STUDIO. PHOTO BY DAVID WHITE

PHOTO BY TIFFANY MARSHALL   PHOTO BY WENDY VECCHI

10 best solutions for PAPER STORAGE

1 Flat file drawers

2 Shoe cubbies (best for stacks of cardstock)

3 A pretty (or industrial) trash can (for rolls)

4 Umbrella stand (for rolls)

5 Large-size zipper bags (clip them to cascading skirt/pant hangers)

6 Wooden clothes-drying rack (for rice and tissue papers)

7 Accordion files. (Attach a scrap with the color to the front of each slot or write the name of the color with a permanent marker.)

8 Archival boxes

9 Plastic protector sheets (magazine cutouts, paper motifs, small images on found papers)

10 Portfolios for extra-large pieces of paper (You can slide the whole thing under the bed.)

6 ways to use PRINTER'S trays

- Found objects
- Jewelry parts and/or beads
- Artist Trading Cards
- Buttons
- Thread
- Mementos

5 neat ways to keep PAINT BOTTLES handy

- On a lazy Susan
- In a spice rack
- Lined up on narrow shelving
- In card-catalog drawers
- In flat-bottomed plastic trays

"I use a cerulean-blue pair of antique shutters upside down so that photos can be held in the slots."

— LOU McCULLOCH, FABRIC ARTIST

PHOTO BY LESLEY RILEY

PHOTO BY JULIANA COLES

5 FABRIC storage solutions

- Stacked on shelves (painted or nonwood to avoid discoloration)
- In see-through plastic bins
- On bolts
- In laundry baskets (good for scraps)
- Stacked in vintage (nonwooden) bowls

5 ways to ORGANIZE your FABRICS

- By color
- By value
- By type of fabric
- By use
- Randomly (especially scraps— you might discover a surprising combination)

5 best ON-THE-GO storage solutions

- Jewelry roll-style wrap for pencils
- Mascot Tutto Machine on Wheels Sewing Carrier Case (tutto.com)
- Plastic zipper bags
- Tackle box
- Fabric tote bags

5 best containers for LITTLE TINY THINGS

- Magnetic containers
- Screw drawers from the hardware store
- Muffin tins
- Mandala game boards
- Egg crates

Corral ODDLY SHAPED OBJECTS in:

- Coin sleeves held in three-ring binders (best for small, flattish bits)
- Garbage cans (best for big, bulky things)

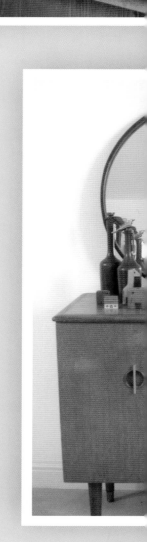

chapter 3
FLEA MARKET FLAIR

"I have literally surrounded myself with all the inspiration and prettiness that makes me feel happy, invigorated, and constantly creative."
— HOLLY A. STINNETT

Do you think objects look better when they're old, grungy, and chipped? Do you often pick up objects left by the side of the road because they have "potential"? Does the word "patina" send a little shiver of excitement down your spine? Then no doubt you're a lover of all things vintage.

It's no surprise many artists find joy in the things other people have cast away. They respect and adore objects that are handcrafted with layers of paint or rust that appeal to the artist's eye. Plus, what could be more creative than taking something once used for one purpose and turning it into something useful again?

Collecting flea market finds can be a thrifty way of outfitting your studio. A little paint here, some TLC there, and someone else's trash becomes your repurposed treasure. Vintage collectibles and accents can also help you personalize your creative space, making it uniquely you.

The artists in this chapter have repurposed just about everything, from transforming a dumpy former movie theater into a dazzling studio on a limited budget to turning an old cast-off frame into a retro-chic inspiration board—and a whole lot in between.

from dump
to divine

by **BRENDA BRINK**

logansport, indiana

Every time I open the door to my studio, I swear I hear a choir of angels singing "Hallelujah." My studio is my sanctuary, a place where I can create to my heart's content, a piece of art in and of itself.

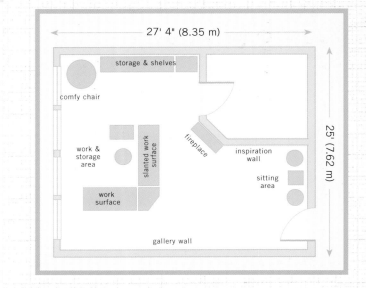

bbrink5@hotmail.com

I am a wife, a mother of seven (ages eleven to thirty-seven), and a grandmother of two. I create in watercolor, collage, assemblage, and mosaic, but it wasn't until I was blessed with my studio that I felt I could add "artist" to that list of titles. After years of being a working mom-artist in my dining room or a small space in my kitchen (next to the washer/dryer—doesn't do much for the creativity), I made up my mind to find a space that I could dedicate to art without the domestic surroundings. The time was right, as all of the kids were in school or out of the house. I was finally able to put my creative needs in the forefront.

After dropping the children off at school, I would drive around town looking at buildings in the hope that one would someday be my studio. The search included a lot of miles, phone calls, and walking through most of the available space in town, but the effort paid off.

BRENDA'S STUDIO

GET ORGANIZED:

Hollow-core doors on top of garage-sale cabinets create two large desks.

A secondhand tea cart becomes a portable paint station.

A black-and-white color scheme is a restful, uncluttered backdrop for art.

Brenda chose a black-and-white palette that wouldn't compete with her art, with pops of yellow to inspire creativity.

When I found my studio it was a dump. But the light was flowing through a wall of windows, and I knew this was the place for me. My studio-to-be was in a two-story old building with some historic significance. It once housed the Paramount movie theater and the sign is still there. My space is on the second floor and, yes, there are twenty-seven steps on the stairway to heaven. I spent a year cleaning, painting, and scraping and sanding the floors. Sweat equity was my rent payment for the first year. Because I spent so much time on my hands and knees working on the floor, I had a lot of time to plan and decorate my studio in my mind.

I searched bookstores and the library for anything that might give me some direction in putting a studio together. Nothing! I eventually chose a white-and-black color scheme because I didn't want anything to fight with my art. I started collecting frames, mirrors, and black-and-white objects from garage sales, flea markets, and thrift shops. I added some yellow because it encourages creativity, and it adds a great pop of color against the black and white. The wall of frames adds texture, and the mirrors reflect light. My two art desks are built from cabinets that I purchased at garage sales, and they are topped with hollow-core doors. My rolling paint station is a secondhand tea cart with plenty of room for brushes, paints, palettes, and supplies. The inspiration wall continues to inspire me and reaffirm what is in my heart. A corner of my studio is designed as a quiet space where I can read, dream up more art, and take a moment to be thankful for the blessing of this studio.

There was no fireplace in the studio space, but the way the wall jutted out it just seemed to beg for one. I brought home a used mantel and put a mirror mosaic inside. With candles aglow, it presents a warm and welcoming focal point and provides a conversation piece for everyone who sees it.

Much to my family's chagrin, my studio does not stay contained within these walls. When at home, my work still takes over the kitchen and the dining room—and don't even think about putting a car in the garage! ✷

above: The dollhouse was a kit that I purchased at a garage sale for 25 cents. While assembling, I knew this had to be a miniature art studio that resembled mine, with tiny frames on the wall, a mirror-mosaic fireplace, a shelf of art books, an art desk, and a gallery. My kids thought I had lost my mind, but I had a ball.

top drawer

file this under "dream come true"

by **WENDY VECCHI**

oglesby, illinois

Welcome to Studio 490. Grab a cup of coffee and I'll give you a tour. But, before we start, let me tell you how this room came to be. I am a full-time artist and stamp designer.

studio490art.blogspot.com

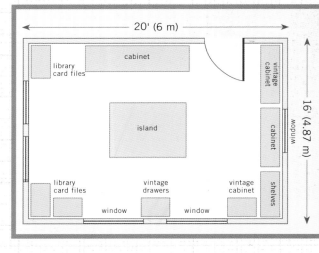

PHOTOS BY WENDY VECCHI

Before we added the studio, I worked in the kitchen and dining area. We started collecting library card file cabinets to store my supplies and stacked them in the dining room. It worked well, and I accomplished a lot, but there were always art supplies on the counter. Then, as I accumulated more supplies, I expanded to the dining room table. As we were standing at the counter eating one evening, my hubby said that we should add a studio, just for me. I remember thinking, "How sweet," when in reality, the poor guy just wanted to sit down and eat! So, several years ago we added Studio 490. Before the construction started, I considered the things that were important to me:

1 Good natural lighting. So, there are five windows and four skylights. Since we live in the country, I kept the window treatments to a minimum.

2 A large working area so I could spread out and plenty of counter space for works in progress.

WENDY'S STUDIO

3   **A sink ... I'm really messy.**

4   **A place for my sewing machine.**

5   **A convenient place for my Genesis paper trimmer.**

6   **Plenty of electric outlets.**

7   **Plenty of storage.**

8   **Easy-to-clean flooring . . . see #3!**

9   **A place to display my art and art from friends.**

With list in hand, we started construction. Six weeks later, I had the studio of my dreams.

The studio is right off the kitchen. It features a 4' × 5' island where I do the major portion of my art.

Since I stand most of the time, it is counter height. But, I also wanted the option to sit when doing handsewing, so there's an overhang on the right side at seat level. Inside the island are pull-out drawers that house the majority of my rubber stamps.

Being organized is a priority for me. I find that if I put things away and always in the same place, I waste less time hunting for them. And, I love to organize. If I'm not making art or shopping, I am quite happy to rearrange something in the studio.

I chose not to have my studio closed off by a door, so the room décor had to fit in with the look of our home. I also wanted my supplies readily available but not out in the open. These cabinets are perfect for me; they go with my country style, and I can store everything in them, from chipboard to paint dabbers. The cabinet and drawer directly behind the island give me easy access to my ink pads, perfect for a rubber stamper.

opposite: The island is where Wendy creates most of her art.

below right: A custom sewing machine cover with chipboard letters spelling "stitch."

One of my favorite pieces is my sewing machine cover. I wanted to have my machine out, but I didn't want to look at that shiny white thing all the time. Luckily for me, my brother is a carpenter and he made a custom cover. It's just a simple wooden box with a cutout for the electric cord. I painted it black, added a vintage handle, and then painted and stamped the chipboard letters "stitch." It's exactly what I wanted, and I love it.

The cabinet on the bottom of this stack belonged to my mother. As we hunted at flea markets and antique malls, we were lucky to find some stackable pieces for a perfect fit—another favorite antique mall find. It holds all my brads, eyelets, jump rings, etc. My embellishment drawer makes me smile: a girl can never have too many embellishments.

I love my studio and my art so much; sometimes I sneak out there in my nighty—but please don't tell anyone. ✺

a little
JEWEL BOX

by **HOLLY A. STINNETT**

los angeles, california

I am a mixed-media artist, a painter, collage artist, seamstress, jewelry maker, journaler, illustrator, blogger, decorator, instructor, and student, and I have a list a mile long of other skills I will tackle in my lifetime.

PHOTOS BY HOLLY A. STINNETT, MARYALENA SALMAN, AND MINDI LIPSHULTZ

My canine companion, Albie, is always by my side, sprawled out on my pink fluffy rug or under my feet catching glitter in his fur or getting paper scraps attached to his nose. My art studio is filled with light, love, and happy energy and is such a fun place to "just be" and create until my heart's content.

Two years ago, my dream came true when we moved into a 1930 Spanish-style home. As soon as I saw one of the small bedrooms, I knew it would make the perfect art studio. I remember sketching out how I would arrange all the furniture to make it fit . . . and it barely did. I had also been envisioning a Tiffany shade of blue for the walls since aqua is one of my favorite colors and an inspiration for my artwork. The color is cheery and playful, yet sophisticated—exactly what I had hoped for. In less than one week, everything was up, displayed, and looking just as sparkly as I had imagined it.

I have literally surrounded myself with all the inspiration and prettiness to make me feel happy, invigorated, and constantly creative. My studio contains endless

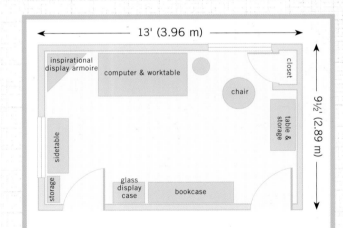

HOLLY'S STUDIO

right: Bookshelves double as a display case for Holly's many vintage treasures.

GET ORGANIZED:

File images by category in a painted wooden box.

Let pretty display items double as storage.

Use custom furniture to hold supplies.

vintage finds, customized and repainted furniture, my artwork, art from friends and discovered artists, as well as special items that belonged to my beloved grandmother.

When friends walk into my studio, they gasp and their eyes widen as they try to take it all in. My studio has been called "a little jewel box," "a Candyland adventure," "a treasure trove," and "Aunt Holly's Vintage Shop," to name a few. I get such a thrill out of watching people discover different things, whether it is my felted Bichon Frise collection, handmade and vintage aprons, or my birdcages.

Because my space is small, I have had to be extremely creative in my filing and organizing systems. Pretty and functional go hand in hand in my little studio of big projects! My bookshelves have also doubled as display shelves and my side table houses numerous supplies such as paper and silk flowers, feathers, fabric,

tulle, and so much more. I utilize a pink painted wooden box as my file system for ephemera and images and have them filed by category such as birds, dogs, flapper girls, etc. A lazy Susan holds my adhesives, paintbrushes, scissors, and gesso, and an old cookie tin allows easy access to all my writing utensils. Spending endless hours in my studio has allowed me to be more creative than I ever could have imagined. I am the absolute proof that one does not need a lot of room to have a beautiful yet functional workspace! ✳

right: Holly's vintage birdcages are one of her favorite finds.

nifty, THRIFTY
renovation meets retro finds

by **LUCIE SUMMERS**

suffolk, england

I'm a terribly untidy person—I get so immersed in my work that paper and fabric scraps pile up around my feet, paints get opened and the lids dropped, and paintbrushes become stiff with dried paint (and kept in a jumble because we all know they make interesting mark-making tools).

before

before

summersville.etsy.com/

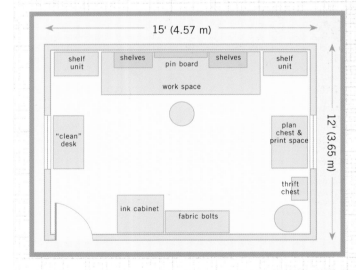

after

PHOTOS BY LUCIE SUMMERS

With all this in mind, when we moved into our new house, I knew I had to have a space that was both inspirational and easy to keep clean. I was very lucky because the farmhouse we moved into (my husband's childhood home) required total renovation. This meant that my studio was custom-built for me. It has two aspects—one looks onto the farmyard, which is not the prettiest of vistas, but lets me see all the comings and goings of farm life—which is important because I'm terribly nosy! The other lets me gaze into the "cottage garden," which will one day be a beautiful floral oasis, but at the moment is a patch of bare grass with a half-empty paddling pool.

One of the best things about my space in our newly built extension is the heated ceramic floor. It has the unexpected perk of serving as a terrific place to dry my fabric, and ink spills can be mopped up quickly and easily.

I have to admit, though, until recently I've only made do in this lovely light-filled room. I didn't have a desk that was large enough for working—so if I wanted to use my sewing machine, I'd have to put my laptop elsewhere (usually on the floor or balancing precariously

LUCIE'S STUDIO

Floor plan labels:
15' (4.57 m)
12' (3.65 m)
shelf unit
shelves
pin board
shelves
shelf unit
work space
"clean" desk
plan chest & print space
thrift chest
ink cabinet
fabric bolts

after

"On one of my thrift-store rummages, I was lucky enough to find an ornate gold frame that I made into a pin board using cork and hot pink spray paint" (see top left image, page 76).

— LUCIE

after

on a bolt of fabric). I had too many nonworking printers/laptops/photocopiers taking up valuable space on another desk and a few huge unpacked boxes from the move loitering along the walls. An enormous wardrobe stood crouched in the corner, a nasty pine monstrosity, full of plastic boxes of fabric and art supplies. Things had to change.

So . . . the first thing I did was order a three-meter long worktop. I had it fixed to the back wall and placed a large wooden shelving unit at each end. The worktop gives me space to keep my laptop out and is also a great "dry" area for drawing and crafting. It has an enormous space underneath for hiding things I want to keep but don't need to access every day. But, of course, all this "stuff" needs a pretty façade to hide behind because see-through stackable boxes are practical but not exactly beautiful. So I purloined (read: "stole") a stash of Kaffe Fassett fabric scraps from my mum—and set about making a cheerful patchwork border for a curtain . . . expertly helped by my quilt-maker mum!

I then bought some floating shelves, cream-colored

baskets, and wooden boxes for storing essentials on my two wooden shelving units. The whole room is a total jumble of thrifted furniture, colorful artwork and interesting pieces from the 1960s and 1970s displayed in a visually pleasing way. I think you'd call my style eclectic! My screen-printing surface is actually an old 1930s plan chest I bought from Cambridge University. It's huge and is brilliant for storing work and hiding a ton of stuff. My printing ink is kept in a thrifted cabinet from the 1960s, and I recently bought a cute chest of drawers that will be great for storing paperwork. It has a sweet little mirror, and I like to have a vase of blossom sitting on it just to look pretty. On another of my thrift-store rummages, I was lucky enough to find an ornate gold frame that I made into a pin board, using cork and hot pink spray paint. It's perfect for pinning up work in progress and little notes and drawings.

I'm thrilled with my new studio and it's a lovely, lovely place to spend time—but just don't expect me to be organized enough to know where I've put anything! ✳

LUCKY LUCIE: HER ETSY "OPEN STUDIOS" EXPERIENCE

In May 2009, designer Lucie Summers was lucky enough to have the coveted "featured seller" spot on the online handmade-goods site, Etsy.com. The exposure on the site's home page was a bit like having a virtual open studios tour, in that visitors could get to know Lucie better and also browse her merchandise. We asked her about the experience.

How did you come by the "featured seller" honor?

I got a total surprise email from one of the Etsy administrators saying they loved my work and asking if I would like to be featured on the Etsy home page. I was in total shock for about an hour—and there was nobody home to tell!

What kind of feedback did you get? How was it different from the feedback you get from your blog, website, or Etsy store?

The feedback I received was so positive. Random strangers got in touch to say how they'd enjoyed the interview and how much they liked my work. It was astounding really. I enjoyed every minute of being in the limelight!

Did anything come from it, such as more sales, a job, higher self-esteem?

I got lots and lots of sales over the two days I was featured, and I had a fantastic couple of months sales-wise afterward, too. It was like a snowball effect—I was featured on lots of blogs, which then resulted in more sales. It was crazy, but really good crazy. I've also had lots of wholesale enquiries in the United Kingdom and United States since, which I'm working on now.

Have you ever participated in a "live" open studio event? How does it compare to a virtual open studio?

I've not done an "Open Studios" event, but I have done demonstrations at The Festival of Quilts exhibition in Birmingham. It's nice to see people face to face, but it's much easier to fill orders in your pajamas! Obviously with a virtual studio event you need to be much more descriptive—people can't touch your goods, so you have to have terrific photographs and the relevant information to help them make their purchase.

What advice would you give to other artists who want to give their work more exposure, but maybe can't do a "live" open studios event?

Never underestimate the power of design/quilting/sewing blogs. Most writers and editors are always interested in new designers and their contact information is readily available on their sites. Social networking sites are great for promotion, I use Twitter quite often to let my followers know about new products, and I write my own blog, too, at blu-shed.blogspot.com. It's a great way to connect with other like-minded people. I also use Flickr (flickr.com/photos/lusummers) to share photos of my work with others. You must read Flickr's terms and conditions carefully, though, and not blatantly link to your work for sale. You can, however, link to your blog, which can then mention where your work is available to purchase.

organizing
with vintage collectibles

by **SUSAN BORGEN**   rowayton, connecticut

Lift the shades and open the windows wide; it's time to fill your studio with fresh air and sunshine. Lighten the mood and let those warm summer breezes waft through your work space.

tpartyantiques.com

Celebrate the leisurely rhythms of the season by bringing the outdoors into your studio through the use of vintage objects and found treasures. Head to an outdoor flea market, garage sale, or neighborhood thrift shop and search for items that reflect a relaxed, carefree spirit. Objects such as pottery vases, flowerpots, and picnic tins can be creatively adapted and reused as storage in your studio.

Summer vacation is the perfect time to take a walk along the beach and collect natural elements such as sea glass, driftwood, polished stones, and shells. When displayed in your work space, these discoveries will add a beachy vibe and keep those vacation memories alive. Or simply head out the back door and stroll through your garden to bring in fresh-cut flowers and terra-cotta pots filled with vibrant blooms.

Display your newfound treasures and use them to round up and store supplies in your studio. These compositions, combining beauty with functionality, will be lovely to look at and are sure to provide you with inspiration all season long. ✳

opposite: **Discover new uses for everyday objects:** A wire flower frog is a playful and practical way to organize paintbrushes. A leafy vintage planter corrals tubes of paint, while an art pottery vase holds a bouquet of brushes. An additional vase contains another bouquet—a bunch of tulips, fresh from the garden.

above left: **Use natural elements and the colors of summer** A sea foam green footstool does double duty as a miniature table to create different levels for an artful display. Whimsical vintage sand pails and old blue Mason jars hold studio supplies. Beautiful shells and sea stars bring the beach home.

above right: **Work with old and treasured objects** Summertime is picnic time: spread out your favorite floral tablecloth and stash supplies in charming old picnic tins. Keep knitting needles close at hand in a pretty vase. A sunshine yellow primrose resides in a vintage flowerpot. Another pot holds bits and ends of yarn. With the addition of clothespins, a discarded wooden trellis found by the side of the road is transformed into a bulletin board.

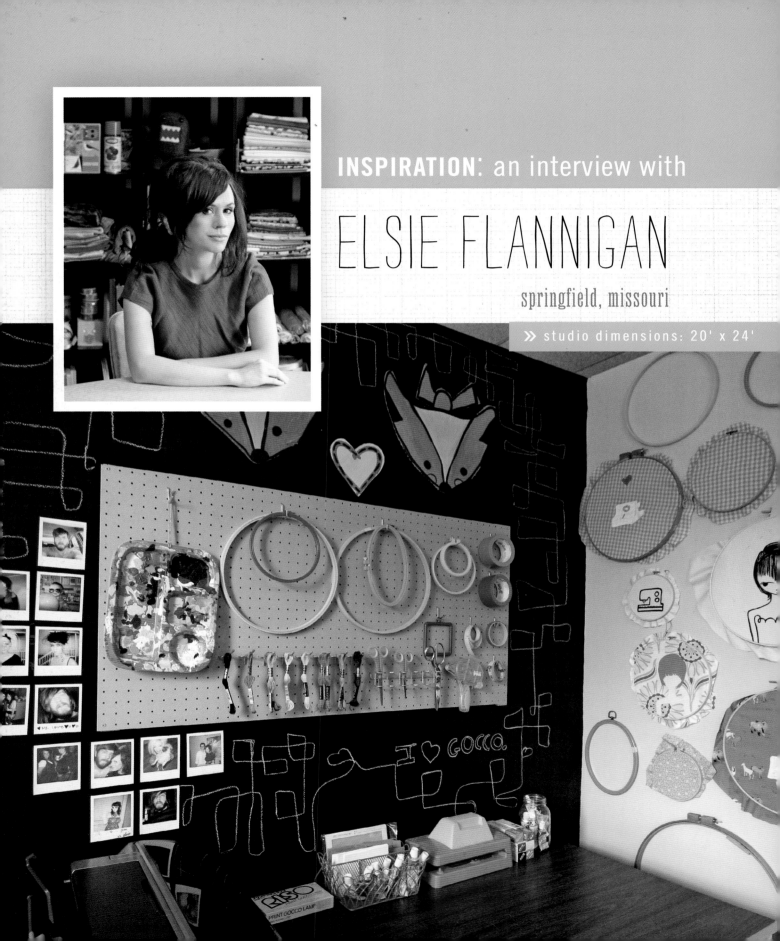

INSPIRATION: an interview with

ELSIE FLANNIGAN

springfield, missouri

» studio dimensions: 20' x 24'

abeautifulmess.typepad.com

PHOTOS BY ELSIE FLANNIGAN

what I do: Full-time independent artist and boutique owner.

why my space works for me: I own an online art boutique and a local store, and a large percentage of my inventory starts in my home studio, so it's a very busy place.

I have a separate studio for painting, so the space you see here is primarily used for sewing and crafting. I adore 1950s and 1960s fashion, hand embroidery, instant cameras, and collecting pretty things.

My studio is always changing. I move from project to project often, so I love that the space is big and open. I like to leave my unfinished projects out while I think about them.

I have a pegboard for most of my stitching stuff and keep my vintage fabric collection in wire baskets. I love working with vintage and recycled materials whenever possible. My yarn is color coordinated. I store all of my plastic "toy" cameras together on a shelf in my studio.

MY FAVORITE THINGS

My modern comic-style illustrations and handstitched accessories.

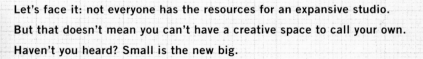

> "I have had much larger homes and studios, but the reality is that I didn't produce any better just because my space was bigger."
>
> — ROBERTA L. PHILBRICK

chapter 4
SMALL SPACE / BIG STYLE

Let's face it: not everyone has the resources for an expansive studio. But that doesn't mean you can't have a creative space to call your own. Haven't you heard? Small is the new big.

If space is at a premium where you live, don't despair. The studios in the following pages will show you that you can make a studio anywhere from a cupboard or closet to a small high-rise apartment. You just have to know how to make the most of the space you have.

It takes planning and determination, but you're up for it, right? As you look through the studios and the tips presented here, note how the artists haven't sacrificed attractive design for efficiency. Also notice how they have cleverly used found and repurposed objects as well as the latest storage and organization products to maximize their space.

With their examples and your ingenuity, you can make your small space into a creative space, too!

in a nutshell

a small space dedicated to creativity

by **JANICE AVELLANA**

honolulu, hawaii

When I first began Hazelnut Cottage in 2007, my art studio consisted of a chair and a small computer desk behind our dining table. Three and a half years later, my art studio is a little bigger. It includes three tables, a large pegboard wall, four stacked cubbyholes, and a wonderful Japanese-style *tansu*.

JANICE'S SMALL SPACE TIPS:

1 Keep supplies out in the open so the work is ready when you are.

2 Disguise a small open studio behind a tall bookcase.

3 For flexible organization, use painted pegboard.

hazelnutcottage.etsy.com

Because Hazelnut Cottage began as a small line of hand-stamped silver jewelry, my space requirements were minimal. However, as my business and space have grown, so has my love for other kinds of art, and I am now delving into mixed media and painting. This has changed my studio needs dramatically. I've found that two fairly simple things have helped me: having lots of open storage and display space and work areas dedicated to specific tasks.

In order to feel inspired and productive, I need to have as many things out on display as possible. Seeing my books, paints, brushes, finished artwork, and photographs of my children helps entice me to come into the studio to play. In the past, I had to work on the dining room table and would have to clean everything up when I was done at night. It took me a long time to realize that one of the reasons I so often wasn't in the mood to work was simply because the setup and cleanup were such huge productions. Keeping my supplies out in the open and being able to leave unfinished projects out has increased my productivity immensely.

Over time, I reorganized my art studio behind a set of tall bookcases, essentially creating a separate room, a dedicated niche that doesn't need to be cleaned up in time for the next meal—hooray! With the help of a baby gate to keep the little ones out during work hours, I set up three work zones. I now have one section dedicated for my computer and paperwork, another section for

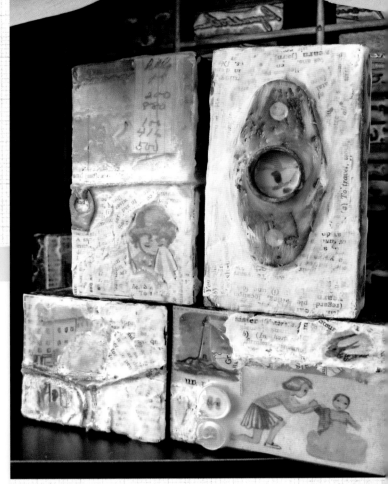

PHOTOS BY ANTHONY VALLEJO-SANDERSON

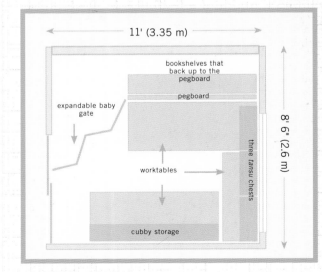

JANICE'S STUDIO

A pegboard wall is a visual organizational tool for Janice.

jewelry making, and a third section for all of my painting and mixed-media projects.

My favorite organizing element is my brand-new pegboard wall. I painted it a pretty robin's egg blue and doodled on it, adding a chalkboard banner at the top so that I can change the words whenever the mood strikes. The pegboard wall is cheery and keeps my important papers in sight, which has proven to be the only system that works for keeping up with my orders and deadlines. In the past, I've tried hanging folders, stackable trays, and binders to keep me organized, but none of those strategies worked. Because I'm such a visual person, being able to see everything helps keep me sane and happy. The wall is also a great place for me to display artwork, and the removable pegs make it easily change-able. I can reorganize the entire wall in just a few minutes! ✳

Janice's studio has three work zones: computer and paperwork, jewelry making, and painting and mixed-media projects.

room
of REQUIREMENT

by **LIZA JULIEN**

salt lake city, utah

My studio was initially set up to coax the artist in me to come out and play. First, I made a large floral fabric and ribbon-covered board to display inspirational images and quotes, then added fun coordinating colored containers for storage.

LIZA'S SMALL SPACE TIPS:

1 Maximize space by going vertical with ladder-style shelving.

2 Store papers suspended from pant hangers on a wooden dowel.

3 Install hooks on table legs, the sides of shelving—anywhere that's handy and out of the way.

lizajulienart.com

PHOTOS BY LIZA JULIEN

I have always loved art and creating, but somehow "got practical" and pursued a degree in materials engineering and, later, a master's in architectural studies. It took some soul-searching and serious studio nesting to get back to art.

As my studio emerged, so did the artist in me, and I started creating art in 2009. I discovered that my preferred art form was collage—which fully explained why, since childhood, I had always felt compelled to collect anything and everything that had color, pattern, texture, or just "had possibilities."

The studio evolved to be more functional and accommodate my accumulation of found materials and art media. A nine-drawer file cabinet holds found papers (colored, patterned, textured), images, texts, maps, and one drawer called "Filling the Well," for inspiration. At my worktable, a carousel holds tools within easy reach, metal baskets hold various media and handmade stamps, and trays hold media and paints. A rolling cart provides a place for my paper cutter, boxes of scrap papers still too good to throw away, stamp-making tools, and my freezer-paper-wrapped bricks for weighing down glued collage elements. IKEA rolling drawers hold stamps, ink pads, stencils, tapes, scissors, punches, and smaller supplies.

I maximized the space further by going vertical. Two ladder-style shelves hold substrates, more supplies, and baskets of textures. Two additional shelving units hold art books, magazines, office supplies, and boxes or

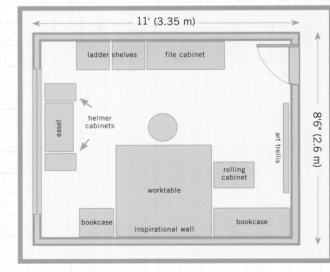

LIZA'S STUDIO

IKEA rolling drawers hold stamps, inks, tape, and other supplies.

stacks of found materials. A wall shelf installed along the length of one wall holds bulkier found materials organized in boxes and various repurposed containers. A wood dowel threaded through the shelf brackets provides a place to hang tissue and handmade papers clipped to pant hangers. My rolling tractor chair allows me to spin seamlessly from my work area to the various storage pieces to access materials or art media.

I designed and built a wooden trellis to hang my artwork on in its various stages. I use wooden clothespins to hang unframed work on canvas board or paper, and S-hooks for framed pieces. The trellis is very handy when working on a series of artwork. Having all the pieces up allows me to see how they are developing. When I get stuck, I can put them up and away and continue to work on new pieces while waiting for that perfect bit of inspiration that will complete each unfinished piece. ✳

Liza's rolling red tractor chair (bottom right corner) allows her to
move quickly and freely to all areas of her studio.

the LOVE shack

where art thrives in a small space

by **ROBERTA L. PHILBRICK**

raleigh, north carolina

This past year we downsized our home and moved into what we affection-ately call "The Love Shack"—all 687 square feet! This means that I no longer have a separate home studio, as I have for the past fifteen years. But that has not stopped me from being able to create daily and write all about it on my two blogs.

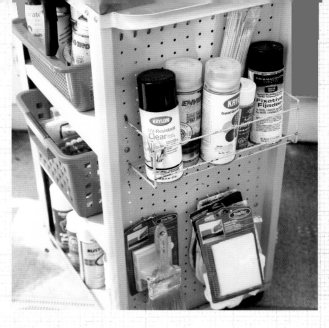

con-tain-it.typepad.com

PHOTOS BY NATALIE ROSS

ROBERTA'S SMALL SPACE TIPS:

1 Use "regular" furniture to hold art supplies.

2 Color-coordinated caddies keep small items organized, portable, and attractive.

3 A glass-topped table cleans up easily and looks polished in a small living/creating space.

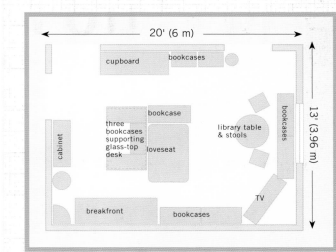

ROBERTA'S STUDIO

My studio is now incorporated into the main living area, which measures 15' × 13'. Currently, my favorite furniture piece is my desk, which I created out of three IKEA bookcases and a piece of glass that used to go on my dining room table. With only two of us in the house, we no longer eat at the table, so I repurposed the glass for my new desktop. This glass top has been a blessing because it takes so much abuse and cleans up fast and easy and still looks nice in this area.

This desk offers such great storage because the dimensions of the cubby sections hold my favorite Memory Keeper paper organizers (acid-free, polypropylene holders sold in scrapbooking stores). I use them to sort my papers by function, project, and/or paper type, e.g., cardboard, mat board, vellum, tag books, collage stickers, etc.

The key for me has always been to designate a function to a container and label everything. The functions and the labels can and do change as my interests and/or projects change. Within twelve cubbies, my desk also stores all of

my pink, green, and black coordinating scrapbook storage cases. These cases hold plastic caddy-type organizers that I use to sort all the ephemera that I have gathered over the years.

Next to my desk is a china cupboard that also has been repurposed for my studio. The bottom open shelves hold my favorite fabric baskets, to which I've added round key-ring tags onto the built-in fabric tabs to clearly label their functions, e.g., adhesives, stencils and masks, sewing, journaling stamp sets, etc. On the top open shelves, you'll find many art journals that I'm working in as well as some very functional green and red wood bins that hold many blank books, journals, and memory albums. To keep my desktop clutter free, I use glass apothecary jars and vessels to hold my paints and fibers. Then I store unsightly objects behind the closed doors of my china cupboard. Supplies such as my art journaling pens and markers are sorted and stored vertically inside a bright green organizer. My current project notebooks are placed on another shelf, with my accordion files full of art clippings for my collage art.

My supplies are stored everywhere here at the Love Shack! So do not assume when you are looking at a piece of furniture that it functions normally. Next to my desk is another small black bookcase that actually sits in the living room side of the room and functions as an end table. But, on the shelves, I store photo boxes that have been repurposed to hold my many paints. I sort by color as well as by type: acrylic, fabric, etc.

The two black ladder shelves hold boxes for wood-mounted rubber stamps, photos, and office supplies. The open backs of these shelves give me some much-needed wall space to hang some of my artwork.

Around the corner from the ladder shelves, you will find yourself at the entry for the Love Shack. Here, I store large rolls of specialty papers in an umbrella stand. Then in the foyer I have mounted white cabinets on the wall to maximize every inch of space! Here, I store my clear stamps inside acrylic CD cases. This makes it is easy to identify each set and take them with me to classes and workshops.

We repurposed a sofa table to hold our big-screen TV and scrapbooking supplies. In all of the four tall black bookcases around the living room, more corrugated boxes hold wood-mounted rubber stamps, sewing

above: Key-ring tags attached to fabric baskets allow for easily identifying the baskets' contents.

supplies, and photos. The top shelves hold all my art reference books, historical novels, and completed art journals.

On those days when I need some space or a place to get a new perspective, I just hang out on my patio. Nothing restores your creative juices more than a swing in the hammock! Or, if I'm in the mood, I open up my spray-painting station, get out my stencils, and just experiment and play.

We really are proud of our Love Shack and how resourceful we have become in our use of space. I have had much larger homes and studios, but the reality is that I didn't produce any better just because my space was bigger. I hope this inspires you to get creative now and not wait for a bigger, or better, space. ✴

above left: Specialty papers find a home in an umbrella stand.

studio
in the sky

by SETH APTER

new york city, new york

I live in New York City where space is at a premium and everybody wants more. Given that, I feel very lucky to have a place in my home that has become a dedicated art studio. It hadn't always been that way.

New York City is such an exciting and vibrant place to live. I derive so much inspiration from just walking down the streets. The flip side to that is the overstimulation that sometimes comes as a result. Being able to escape to my very own art retreat in my studio is the perfect balance. I live on a very high floor and have a wall of windows almost six feet high. I have a city view and can see many miles in the distance on a clear day. At night the lights of the city sparkle and shine, providing a glow that seems to fuel my creative energy.

I have set up my studio so that I am surrounded by inspiration on the inside as well. The many cabinets and surfaces all contain ingredients that are waiting their turn to become part of my artwork. I count among my many collections vintage boxes, cabinets, and cases. Some are faded wood, some battered metal, and some distressed leather. All have a distinct patina that serves as a never-ending source of inspiration. They are full of paper scraps, metal finds, and all kinds of other art supplies. Given the large number of small bits and pieces that are the core of my artwork,

thealteredpage.blogspot.com

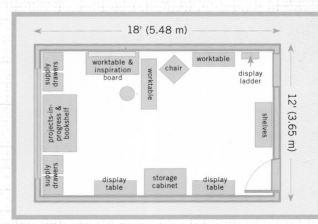

SETH'S STUDIO

I have found a good storage solution in a series of new, multi-drawer, stackable metal cabinets by Bisley. Inside the drawers are trays with different-sized compartments, allowing for easy organization and access (nearly) every time.

I always work on many projects at the same time, both my own and my collaborations, and I have a table dedicated to these works in progress. On other surfaces, you will find completed art projects alongside art that I have acquired from artists and friends whom I admire. I love unusual, one-of-a-kind objects, and these are scattered throughout my studio. Above my main worktable is an inspiration board that I update periodically. On it you will find my own work, gifts that I have received from other artists, ephemera, rusty metal, and other items that keep me creatively charged.

One of my tables is dedicated to my computer, which sometimes seems to be the "art supply" that I use the most as I work to maintain my blog. A comfortable swivel chair is there, too, for when I want to relax with or without my laptop. I am surrounded by art magazines and books, both vintage ones that I use as an art supply as well as new ones that I read for instruction and inspiration. I use a bookcase and the space below a worktable to hold stacks of the new books. The vintage ones are tied into bundles and spread around the studio as part of mini art vignettes.

I view my studio as a work in progress and have plans to make changes over time. New paint colors on the walls and larger worktables are likely to be the next updates. Every so often I get the urge to rearrange the art on my walls and all the "stuff" that fills the nooks and crannies. In this way, my studio becomes almost like a gallery, with ever-changing exhibitions. And this is important to me, as my space is as much a source of inspiration as it is a place to create. ✳

SMALL-SPACE STRATEGIES

- Maximize the space you have by going vertical with shelving and ladder-style storage. Don't forget the space over the tops of windows.

- Install hooks on table legs, the sides of shelving, or anywhere else that will keep supplies handy yet out of the way.

- Know when to fold 'em: Fold-down tables, counters, and ironing boards are great space savers.

- Make collectibles such as vintage suitcases or milk glass vases do double duty as storage containers.

- Look out below: Store supplies beneath counters and tables. Attach an attractive fabric skirt to disguise the clutter.

- Use uniform stackable boxes to contain clutter and give the room a clean look.

- Store supplies in baskets hung from the ceiling.

- Have a place "off-site" (such as a basement or storage shed) to keep bulky or seldom-used materials.

- Regardless of size, make it personal, to encourage creativity.

strategic DESIGN

by **MICHELLE SPAW**

kansas city, missouri

When I decided to convert a spare bedroom into a studio, there were several aspects to consider. The room is slightly rectangular, and strategic placement of furniture was a priority.

MICHELLE'S SMALL SPACE TIPS:

1 For an eclectic approach to organizing, try using non-conventional items such as stackable trays, bento boxes, and takeout-style containers.

2 Removing the doors to your closet is a strong incentive to keep it tidy. Because the contents are always visible, you will be motivated to maintain order and curb the clutter.

3 When purchasing storage boxes, think of color and pattern as a way to identify what you're storing: striped boxes to hold striped fabric or ribbon, solid color boxes for solid color twine and embroidery thread, or floral-print boxes for floral-print scrapbook paper.

PHOTOS BY MICHELLE SPAW

michellespaw.com

Because my creative time is divided among collage and painting projects as well as freelance writing assignments, I felt having separate workstations was essential. The long white table 26" × 78" is perfect for mixed-media pieces when I need to spread out items such as canvas panels, an illustration board, or stacks of paper. Next to the long table, a cabinet with shallow drawers and dividers was designed to hold cassette tapes and has been re-purposed to store paintbrushes, hole punches, and small tools. I use a smaller table for my computer and a wire basket to hold file folders, sketchbooks, and calendars. Two rolling carts (one with shelves and one with bins) are easy to maneuver and provide quick access to materials. In order to maximize storage options, I had a custom closet system installed that incorporates built-in drawers, shelves, and cubbies. I use a freestanding chest for paint chips, tags, tissue paper, and assorted scraps.

Wall treatment was another concern due to my philosophy that walls should never be just a backdrop for a space,

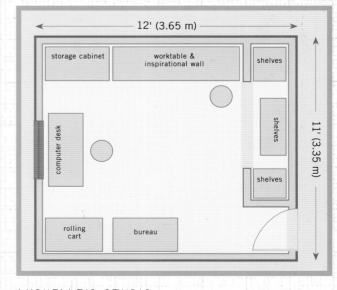

MICHELLE'S STUDIO

below: A freestanding desk houses paint chips, tags, and tissue paper.

but rather an integral part of the overall aesthetic and composition. Although the previous owners of our home had chosen a busy wallpaper pattern for the room, I thought a neutral painted surface was best and would allow displayed elements to have a strong presence without competing with one another. I chose cream and chocolate paint shades that blend well with my personal work and complement reference pieces I have pinned up on a series of bulletin boards.

My feeling is that if you think of your studio space as an extension of your personality and surround yourself with your favorite things, you will constantly be inspired. As part of this philosophy, I like to use interesting boxes and containers for storage.

I know that as my work evolves, my studio will change as well. I like the fact that it's always in a state of transition: constantly being rearranged, reinvented, and rediscovered. ✳

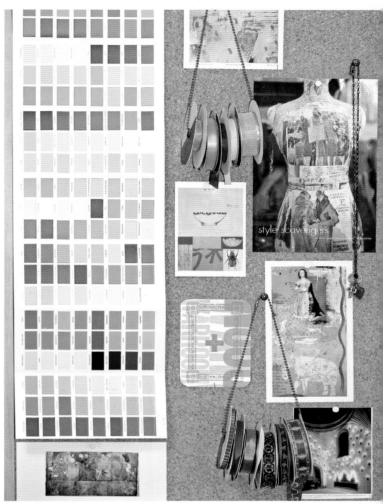

above right: Ribbons hang from a ball chain on a corkboard for easy access.

INSPIRATION: an interview with

GAIL SCHMIDT

butler, tennessee

≫ studio dimensions: 9' x 11'

shabbycottagestudio.blogspot.com

what I do: Mixed-media art

why my space works for me: With two doors, a closet, and windows that take up most of a 9' wall, there is an opening on every wall of my studio, making furniture placement and storage a creative adventure. That has not deterred me, however!

In front of the windows, a worktable runs the entire wall. I like a functional work area and don't want to keep getting up to find things, so the corner on one end is storage for everyday tools and embellishments.

My motto is, if you don't have room to build out, then build up, and shop your home for creative storage ideas. I took a couple of tool caddies and an old wire rack turned upside down and attached them to the wall. Clear plastic containers and old dressers make great storage. A chest of drawers does double-duty storing vintage laces, while I use the top for ironing. Two rolling carts under the table store fabric scraps, stamps, and punches. There is so much I can do in this area with a swivel of my chair. I'm claustrophobic, and the open door took up 3' of space, so I replaced it with an old screen door, which I love.

On the wall at the other end of the table, I gained 6' of space by removing closet doors and adding lots of shelves and another worktable. I now have a spot for sewing, fabric storage, and a reference library. Placing a freestanding paint area at a right angle from the closet creates a convenient U-shaped work area.

Another open door rendered the wall behind it useless until we added 3" shelves that hold small items. Opposite this wall, at a right angle from the door, I placed two storage cabinets. The cabinets and paint table now act like walls and give me a small room within a room. I brought in a tall chest of drawers, plus an old dresser to which I added a bookcase on top. Between these I store a lot of items I use for creating my art. ✸

MY FAVORITE THINGS

My painting table and the 9' worktable, both built for me by my husband.

chapter 5

"Lighting is one of the most important considerations when designing a work space."
— BARBARA DELANEY

THE POWER OF LIGHT AND COLOR

Light is essential to the artist and the art. Light reveals color, shadow, and positive and negative space. The correct lighting also helps to prevent headaches and eyestrain. And when you want to present your artwork through photos (on the Internet or in your portfolio), you need proper lighting to capture the true beauty of your creations.

Color can influence your creativity, your energy, and your state of mind. Some artists prefer a "clean" palette of white to work in, while others need the cheer of warm pinks or the zing of a bright blue.

In this chapter, we enlighten you with how to find the right lighting for you and your studio as well as your art. The studios featured here show how to take advantage of natural light and how color can lift your spirit and invigorate your imagination.

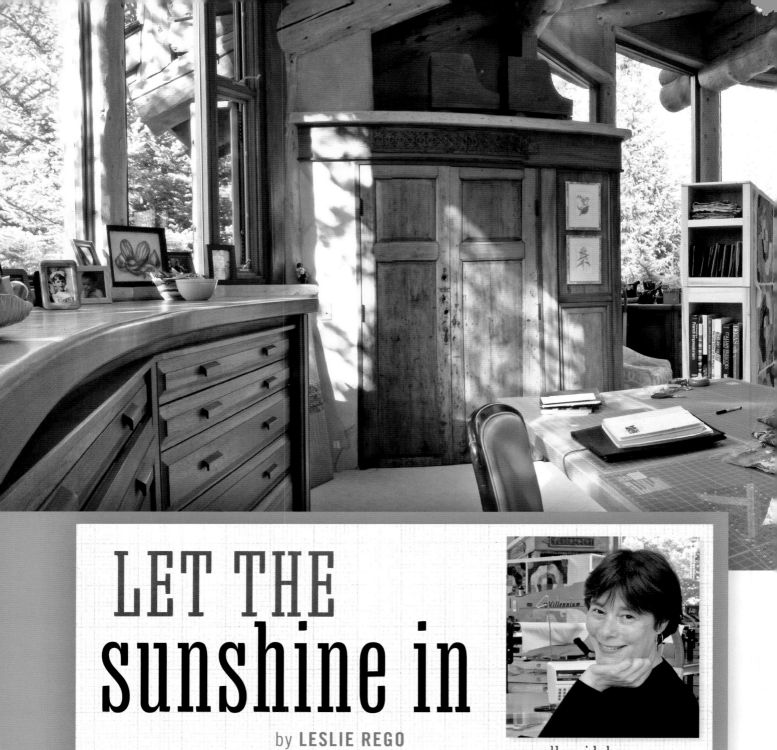

LET THE
sunshine in

by **LESLIE REGO**

sun valley, idaho

My husband, our three children, and I moved to Sun Valley, Idaho, from Guatemala twenty-two years ago. We chose to live here because we love the mountains and Sun Valley's open space.

I designed my quilt studio with these ideas in mind: lots of open floor area, views of the Sawtooth National Forest from tall windows on all four sides of the room, and furniture that is easy to move to be able to follow the sun around the room throughout the year.

I have a sitting area with a fireplace to enjoy the winter days when the sun sets early. My sewing machine tables are easy to reconfigure in different spots of the room, allowing me to work with the warm winter sun on my back or to enjoy a shady spot during the summer months. My large worktable moves up and down, so I can be comfortable both standing and sitting.

Most of the woodwork in my studio was custom-made. The doors are old doors from Guatemala that we refinished. My design wall is a freestanding structure

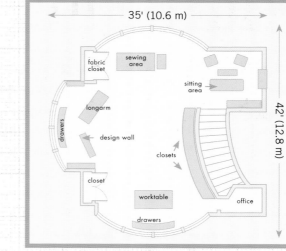

LESLIE'S STUDIO

that I can move around the room, depending on the sun's position at any given month. Using both sides of the wall, I can design two large quilts at the same time. The design wall has bookshelves nestled into the ends that are handy for oversized art books and for rolls of fabric. I store all of my PFD (prepared for dyeing) fabric there.

I like to keep my threads and my collection of old laces and trims in drawers so that they stay out of the sun and do not collect dust.

The old black Singer sewing machine was my mother's. She sewed all of her clothes with it as well as my childhood dresses. Eventually, she bought a new machine and passed this one along to me. For years, using this well-loved sewing machine, I made couture clothing for myself along with my first few quilts.

My favorite chair in the studio is an antique Guatemalan armchair that I had recovered with a purple Guatemalan ikat fabric (see photo, opposite, top left)

I have a Pilates machine in my work space so that I can stretch and ease out the kinks after I have been working for a while.

Above the stairs is a small loft area that I use as my office. ✳

leslierego.com

LESLIE'S
TIPS AND HINTS:

1 If space allows, have furniture that is easy to move so you can follow the sun around the room throughout the year.

2 Purchase or retrofit a table that can move up and down so you can use it while sitting or standing.

3 With a two-sided, freestanding design wall, you can work on two full-size quilts (or other projects) at once.

PHOTOS BY F. ALFREDO REGO

above: Most of the woodwork in Leslie's studio was custom-made.

living in
COLOR

by **JUDITH CONTENT**

palo alto, california

Art quilter Judith Content began decorating her environment at an early age. For her first project, she covered her bedroom walls with construction paper. Judith still envelops herself with color, but now she uses paint, textiles, art, and found objects. "It comes out of being an artist. I consider my house a gallery of sorts," she says.

JUDITH'S TIPS AND HINTS:

1 Display collections and colorful art materials throughout your home.

2 Use baskets to store materials out of the way and grass mats to cover utilitarian objects and projects in progress.

3 Break the rules. Use your artistic sensibilities to decorate your home in a way that makes you happy.

judithcontent@earthlink.net

ABOVE PHOTO BY ANNE GRAHAM.
ALL OTHER PHOTOS BY JAMES DEWRANCE.

JUDITH'S STUDIO

Judith paints her walls, woodwork, floors, and many pieces of furniture to surround herself with color and to provide a backdrop for the art she collects and creates. The one exception is in her studio. There she has white walls, gray carpeting, and utilitarian surfaces because her materials and artwork are so richly colored. Judith hand-dyes and pieces silk for her art quilts and also paints buttons and papers for collage.

But in the living space, the next painting session is always just around the corner, as Judith is always in pursuit of the perfect combination of hues to complement her art and her life.

"I think in color and I love to paint," she explains. Judith says her husband is fine with her choices, though she does tend to wait until he's traveling to get out the brushes and drop cloth. "But that's because I paint into the wee hours. I paint until I'm done or I like it," she says.

Judith's approach to painting furniture is unconventional. While most people prefer a white, primed "canvas," she starts off with a coat of black acrylic, such as Ceramcoat. She likens the effects she achieves this way to discharge dyeing: you start with black fabric and discharge the color, but the discharged areas never turn to a pure white but rather stay a creamy color. When you over-dye the discharged fabric, the combination with the creamy white results in a more "sensitive" color, she says. Similarly, painting colors over black gives the finished look more of an "eye-catching quality," according to Judith.

Judith uses latex house paint with an eggshell finish

to paint the walls, which results in a glowing patina. To apply the color, Judith uses a kitchen sponge that she has plucked here and there to make the surface uneven. Then she picks up three colors of latex house paint on the sponge—for example, magenta, turquoise, and teal—and spreads on the paint. She experiments as she goes with the ratios of the colors and often dilutes the paint, letting it drip down and streak. Judith adds more layers of color until she is happy with the result, noting that with her method, the under layers of color always come through a little bit—an outcome she desires. The hardwood floors are not exempt from Judith's passion for painting; instead of refinishing them, she whitewashed them with diluted primer.

"Every rule in the book, I break," she says without remorse.

Though she's not shy about splashing color around, Judith's approach to artful home design is hardly slapdash. She brings the same attention to detail to her home as she does to her carefully pieced quilts. Judith loves to create vignettes with her many collections, but she doesn't just amass them. The groupings are always edited by some feature, such as color or gradation of size.

She also looks for ways to layer the collections with a complementary texture or pattern. For example, the vertical sticks in her collection of whisk brooms complement the horizontal lines in the piece of driftwood she uses to display them. And the organic shape of the wire sculpture that sits on a Japanese tansu chest mirrors the structure of the jellyfish motif in the art quilt hanging on the wall above.

"My materials are beautiful, and I love having them out where I can see them," says Judith. Thus, her laundry room doubles as the bead room, where strings of beads hang on the wall or are arranged in bowls like artwork. Judith disguises the functional elements in the room behind woven beach mats, a trick she uses in other parts of the house as well.

For storage in the studio areas, Judith relies on baskets of all kinds. Because she works with strips and pieces of silk, she does not fold her fabrics. She just tosses them into baskets and puts them on a shelf when not in use. She also dyes the fabric she needs, so she rarely buys fabric to use "someday." In that way, she is able to keep her stash under control. "I use it up—but then, I never throw anything away, either," says Judith.

Judith keeps her papers in a large rectangular basket. Tidying up is easier when she doesn't have to sort them, and she's happy to shuffle through them to find the one she needs. She does most of her art painting in her colorful shed. She stores supplies in baskets that hang from the ceiling and on utility shelves that are disguised behind roll-down bamboo blinds. Living in California, she is able to dye outside almost all year-round out by her brightly hued "serape" deck.

Storage in the rest of the house is primarily in Japanese *tansus* she and her husband collect. In fact, much of the couple's furniture doubles as storage, such as boxes with lids that are used as side tables. "Anything that will hold anything probably does," says Judith. In this way, she is able to avoid clutter and put the focus on color.

Recently, Judith's artful home has been featured as a stop on area house tours, and she appreciates the interest.

"It's fun to have people wanting to come and see this unusual home," Judith says. "But I do this for my-self, because I love living in color." ✸

INSIDE THE CREATIVE STUDIO

COLOR YOUR CREATIVITY

**How does your studio's predominant color affect you? Ultimately, it's a personal choice.
But here are some tips for choosing your most creative color scheme.**

WHITE. The classic studio wall color is white because it reflects light and serves as a neutral background to the artist's art. White gives a feeling of openness and airiness but can also feel cold and antiseptic. Warm up white with wood furniture, tools, and trim or choose a white with more yellow and less blue mixed in.

RED. A bold choice, red can be very energizing and stimulating. This effect can boost creativity, but may also send you into overdrive. If red walls are too overwhelming, get your blood pumping with spots of color, such as a red chair or desk accessories.

BLUE. The color of the ocean and the sky is known for being relaxing. But be careful, too much gray in that blue can be a downer, like stormy skies. They don't call it a blue mood for nothing.

GREEN. Another calming color, and one that goes with just about everything, is green. Credit Mother Nature—it's the hue she relies on most. The only downside to green: it can be too relaxing. Don't forget, you want to get some work done in that studio! Zap it with a little yellow if you want more energy.

YELLOW. The color of sunshine and daffodils, yellow is a happy color that can give you an emotional boost when you enter your studio each day. But, like red, it has a dark side: the more intense lemony yellows can irritate and frustrate you, making a bad mood worse. It may be safe to stick to the paler shades or to use yellow as an accent.

PURPLE. The color of royalty and creative people, purple could be the perfect hue for your studio. By turns dramatic, sophisticated, and (in the lighter shades) relaxing—all you need is a crown, and you'll be queen of your creative domain.

yummy goods

a studio within a store serves its designer well

by MELISSA AVERINOS

west barnstable, massachusetts

In the fall of 2008, I opened the gift store I'd been dreaming of for years: Yummy Goods, where I feature locally made soaps, handmade jewelry, household items, books, and handmade accessories using fabric from my Sugar Snap collection for Westminster Fibers/Free Spirit Fabrics. Just a few buildings away from my house in the Cape Cod village of West Barnstable, the store also houses my studio!

yummygoods.com

PHOTOS BY MELISSA AVERINOS

While designing the layout for the retail area of the business, I created a semiprivate section in the rear to serve as my on-site work space. More than solely utilitarian, it is my home away from home, where I often have meals and visit with friends. As such, I wanted it to be cozy and inviting, in addition to having plenty of storage and ample work surfaces for projects.

Painting the walls the same salmon pink as in my living room instantly created the warm feeling I was after. Creative reuse of castoff materials fulfilled the practical requirements.

Two dreary retail display cases were transformed by repainting them a bright white and removing the legs. Pushing the pieces face-to-face created a large tabletop with plenty of hidden storage in the cabinets underneath. My favorite feature of this makeshift table is the

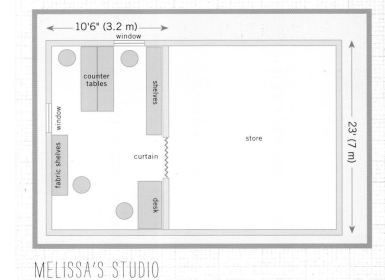

MELISSA'S STUDIO

display area below the glass countertops where I arrange playful vignettes that amuse and inspire me.

Above the repurposed cases hang two large bulletin boards that I covered with the "Tendril" print from my Sugar Snap collection. Here, I pin magazine cutouts, prints of fabric designs in process, found scraps, vintage fabric swatches—anything that visually interests me.

A floor-to-ceiling shelf unit holds my quilting fabric stash. I organize the larger scraps by color to create a sense of order, even though the fabric itself is imperfectly folded. Notions and other supplies are stored in tins and boxes. When I find a sturdy basket at a yard sale, I grab it, give it a coat of white paint, and employ it as an inexpensive and cute place to keep my projects-in-process. Nestled among the fabric stacks, thrift-store

enamel bowls hold ironed pieces ready to be sewn into scrappy quilts.

Working in many different media (and having the studio visible from the shop!) means finding attractive and creative ways to store supplies is a necessity. Any container will be considered, from cigar boxes, tins, and vintage mugs to even (very well-washed) anchovy tins. I keep adhesives and rubber stamps in Clementine crates shelved on white bookcases. Banker's boxes hold collage materials I've collected over the last twenty years; I add to my finds continually.

A small banquet table painted white defines the office area where I work on new fabric collections, edit photos, and write blog posts. Above the computer desk, two doors from an old metal cabinet were given new life

above: Muffin tins are a fun way to showcase beads.

left: Melissa's fabric stash is organized by color on a floor-to-ceiling shelf.

as a magnetic bulletin board where I hang personal photos and notes, event reminders, and positive quotes.

Even in this tiny studio, I made sure that enough floor space remains for lounging with a stack of canvases to paint the day away, lay out fabric for a quilt, or welcome a friend for a chat. Thanks to maximizing the space with hidden storage and displaying practical items in creative ways, not only can I work and play in the studio—it's a pleasure to do so. ✷

FOR YOUR illumination

how to choose the best lighting for your studio

by BARBARA DELANEY

Lighting is one of the most important considerations when designing a work space. Good light is crucial, and the older we get, the more light we need. I spoke to some experts in the lighting field, did some research online, and asked some of our favorite artists for their ideas to help you tackle this all-important job.

opposite and above: Flexible neck lamps put light right where you want it, as seen on Margery Erickson's beading table (opposite) and on Melanie Testa's sewing machine (above).

above right: An Ott-Lite focuses on Belinda Spiwak's beading project.

Though ambient lighting is desirable and attractive in a general living space, all-purpose lighting is not sufficient in areas where visual tasks are performed—sewing, reading, crafts, and even food preparation—and therefore it must be supplemented with additional light sources. Task lighting alone is not comfortable, so a combination of general lighting and task lighting is best.

Susan Arnold, senior designer at Wolfer's Lighting in Waltham, Massachusetts, says that for starters, people need to think beyond the technical aspects of lighting and really consider what will work best for their needs. Someone who paints needs different lighting than someone who is handstitching in her lap—though they both may be working in "studio space." She suggests the best tactic is to flood the room with light and add additional illumination for the task at hand, so you don't create shadows.

Many of the artists interviewed like to have some ambient light to set the mood for creating or to just enjoy their space. But they rely on additional lighting for close work.

HOW TO SELECT GENERAL AND TASK LIGHTING FOR A ROOM

1 Measure the room. When choosing lighting, you will need to take the area of light each fixture provides into consideration.

2 Factor in wall color and natural light sources. Darker walls absorb light; lighter walls reflect it. A south-facing window will let in brighter light than one that is north-facing.

3 Use recessed lights or track lighting to focus light on task areas. Space lights close enough to allow for overlap of lighting areas.

4 Use adjustable lights like eyeball fixtures that can be rotated or redirected to focus on different areas.

5 Before placing lights, take note of where people do various activities. Do they need light from directly overhead? Behind them?

6 Position overhead lights over tables and desks, before mirrors, and around the center of the room.

Sandy James of Design Solutions in Maynard, Massachusetts, works closely with homeowners when creating a lighting plan for their space. Her design is generally used as a guide for the homeowner and electrician, with the exact locations of the lights determined on-site based on structural elements.

A number of things have to be considered when deciding on lighting: the size of the room/space, the height of the ceiling, and the type of lighting you need: task, general, or accent, or all of the above. Sometimes she uses a combination of recessed-can lighting, some track lighting, and pendant lighting if the lamps will hang over a table or island-type work area. James thinks halogen lighting is a good choice for bright task, art, or accent lighting, especially if the size of the space allows for good beam control, and she notes that the CRI (Color Rendering Index) of the chosen bulb must be taken into consideration as well.

Pat Sloan uses flexible task lighting for close work and a floor lamp for general lighting.

PHOTOS BY ALBERT R. SARVIS, MELANIE TESTA, J.G. HALL, BELINDA SPIWAK, GREGG SLOAN, ALMA DE LA MELENA COX, AND SOLUX.

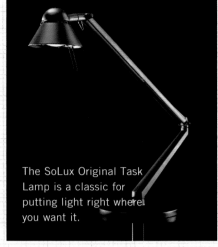

The SoLux Original Task Lamp is a classic for putting light right where you want it.

LIGHTING TERMS

FLUORESCENT — Produces light when acted upon by radiant energy.

HALOGEN — Halogen combines with the tungsten evaporated from the hot filament to form a compound that is attracted back to the filament, thus extending the filament's life. Very bright and warm light.

XENON — Contains xenon gas and no filament. Considered as bright as the noonday sun, cooler in temperature than incandescent lights, but warmer than halogen.

INCANDESCENT — The kind of lightbulb used in most homes throughout the twentieth century. Electric current passes through a thin filament, heating it until it produces light.

FULL SPECTRUM — Produces light that has certain desirable qualities that make it similar to natural sunlight. The brightness value of the light is similar to that of daylight, and the bulbs have excellent color-rendering capability.

CRI (COLOR RENDERING INDEX) — Color rendering is the accuracy of how well a bulb shows the colors it illuminates. The color-rendering index ranges from 1–100, with the higher numbers approaching the color replicating properties of full-spectrum sunlight (sunlight having a CRI rating of 100). Thus, the higher the CRI, the truer colors appear. Look for bulbs rated at least 75 or higher.

Alma de la Melena Cox puts the spotlight on her art with track lighting.

task lighting

Home improvement expert Bob Vila has an excellent guide to room lighting on his website (bobvila.com). For general work, Vila suggests that the best task lighting is diffused and should be placed over the shoulder of the user, or to the side of the work area. But for hobby or close work, the best solution is "down lighting," meaning the light should be concentrated and come from above the work. Tasks that are lit from the front of the user and from above are free of annoying shadows, making attention to detail much easier.

Vila further suggests that to determine how much task lighting will be needed, you need to think about the age of the people using the area, how detail-oriented the task is, and the type of work surface to be used. Are your overhead lights sufficient for general use? If not, how can you improve the lighting? Is reflectance or surface glare going to be a problem? What options are available and will they work in your space? These are some of the questions that need to be asked and answered before moving forward.

Unless you only work in the daytime and in a room with a lot of windows, you need to have good overhead (general) lighting. And, since many artists and crafters work in spare spaces in their homes (such as attics, garages, and basements), additional task lighting is essential. Luckily, there are many bulbs and lamps available that provide good light; many even mimic daylight. These are usually referred to as full-spectrum lighting. Full-spectrum bulbs are available both as standard lightbulbs and as fluorescent tubes. They produce a clear light that is beneficial to anyone who needs to be able to distinguish between color discrepancies. Unfortunately, they do tend to be more expensive than standard bulbs.

A number of different options are available for task lighting. Many people like to use lights with flexible necks so they can be adjusted as needed. Others like "fixed" lights that can be mounted overhead (such as track lighting) or under a cabinet in their work space, such as puck lights (so named because of their size and shape). There are also stand-alone units that usually run the length of the cabinet; these can be plug-in or hardwired. And, there is even a light that fits on your ear like a Bluetooth, providing direct light onto your work.

bulbs

Not only do you have to choose the kind of light/lamp you want, you also have to decide on the type of bulb you want to use. There are four main types: fluorescent, halogen, xenon, and incandescent: You may choose any one kind of light or a combination just be sure that the light source you choose is neither too bright nor too dark and that it is appropriate for the size of the space.

Fluorescent lights are a bright and inexpensive way to illuminate a work space—but don't judge them by their past reputation. According to Joyce Gravel, also of Wolfer's Lighting, fluorescent lighting has come a long way in recent years. The current bulbs are smaller and the fixtures are smaller, too. New technology has minimized the flickering and the hum we all remember, and they draw less energy than incandescent bulbs, making them a greener choice. Gravel says that there has been a lot of resistance to fluorescents over the years, but manufacturers have responded by improving the technology and by introducing decorative fixtures and lamps, often offering stylish lighting that provides both incandescent and fluorescent options.

TIPS FOR AVOIDING EYESTRAIN

Prolonged close work such as handstitching or beading can wreak havoc on your eyes. Having the proper lighting for the task helps, but there are other things you can do to help prevent eyestrain.

BLINK. Sometimes we're so intent on our task we "forget" to blink. But blinking produces tears that help moisten and lubricate the eyes. So make a conscious effort to blink often.

USE PROPER EYEWEAR. If you wear glasses or contacts, be sure your prescription is up to date and appropriate for close work. If you "just" need reading glasses, wear them! Don't forget: squinting causes wrinkles.

TAKE BREAKS. At least once an hour, look up from your close work and focus on something across the room. Stand up and move around, if possible, and lean back and close your eyes for a moment.

RELAX. When you take your eye break, be sure to relax. Let your arms hang loose and drop your chin to your chest. Then, place your elbows on your desk or worktable, turn your palms toward your face, and rest your head in your hands. Breathe slowly and deeply for about thirty seconds. Look up and do a couple of shoulder rolls. Exercises like this refresh your eyes and loosen your neck and shoulder muscles, decreasing fatigue.

Gravel suggests that artists really need to explore the possibilities before settling on lighting for their space, as there are many ways to light a room. For example, halogen lamps provide the most intense light (great for intricate work) and there are indirect fluorescents that provide flat general light that is thrown throughout the room. Wolfer's actually has a lab where people can see how different lights perform in different scenarios.

artists' preferences

Most artists prefer to work in natural light, but that isn't always possible. Fiber artist and art quilter Judy Perez has amazing natural light in her Chicago loft home, but at night it's a different story. As a result, she works mostly during the day and uses an OttLite when she wants to work in the evening and doesn't have that natural light.

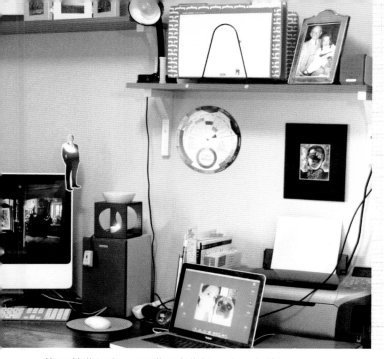

Kass Hall tucks a small task light on her shelf to illuminate her work area.

Art quilter Jamie Fingal rents her studio space and therefore has to work with the existing lighting: fluorescent ceiling lights. She also leaves all of the window shades up to take advantage of as much natural light as possible. For task lighting, she positions a desk-mounted, long-arm OttLite right by her sewing machine and another clip-on light on her design table.

Though fluorescent lighting is a good alternative to natural light, some artists will not use it at all. If she doesn't have daylight, mixed-media fiber artist Melanie Testa prefers regular incandescent bulbs while working. Fiber artist Lesley Riley likes to work with natural light, too, but also uses her overhead room lights and regular incandescent lamps. She also has an OttLite that she employs when she needs extra light.

"The OttLite is small but powerful. I think the fact that it doesn't take up much space and simulates natural light are its two biggest pluses," says Lesley.

Sometimes, natural light can be too much of a good thing. Linda Kemshall's quilting studio is in a separate building in her garden. It's a modest size, but it has a glass roof over half of its length so natural light floods in during the day.

"Sometimes it's too bright, and I have to use blinds to cut the glare," she says.

Linda also has repositional spotlights on two ceiling-mounted tracks so she can alter the direction of the light source whenever she wants. "The spots are great for when I need to concentrate light on a specific area, such as my design wall," she says.

For close work, Linda also has a floor-standing Ott-Lite, which she finds indispensable during the dark days of winter. She positions it slightly behind her armchair with the moveable arm extending over her shoulder and uses it in the evenings "to create a pool of light so I can handsew without disturbing anyone who's watching the TV."

Linda says, "I'm lucky to have an electrician in the family—I tell him what I need, and he tells me how to achieve it!" ✳

my BLUE heaven

by **KATHY YORK**

austin, texas

aquamoonartquilts.blogspot.com

PHOTOS BY KATHY YORK

I had wanted to switch from carpeting to concrete floors for a long time, as I thought it would be a better fit for the casual lifestyle we lead. I finally had it done, and I absolutely love the color of my floors! Isn't it amazing how well it goes with my painted wallpaper? And my art? The color looks totally fabulous with my art quilts.

Aside from the horrendous mess and hard work of moving everything, it was totally worth it. I love my new room. It feels fresh and clean and relaxing! ☀

> "Some people may wonder why someone who paints frequently would choose white tabletops."
>
> — POKEY BOLTON

chapter 6

MAKE IT YOUR OWN

So, now you have the basics: how to find space, how to organize and store, how to make the most of the space you have, how to make light and color work for you.

Now, it's time to make your space your own personal haven, whether you're starting from scratch or are making over an existing space. The artists in this chapter have each made a creative haven to suit their practical and aesthetic needs. Through thoughtful planning, ingenuity, and, in some cases, professional assistance, they have merged their art medium, their organizational preferences, and their style of working to create a studio that suits them perfectly.

From the clean lines of Pokey Bolton's quilt and mixed-media studio to spacious fiber art studios of Margery Erickson and Catherine Nicholls to the funky polka-dot and whimsical faux crown molding of Jennifer Heynen and Kristin Krause's studios, you will see that no matter what your studio style, you can make it your own.

extreme STUDIO makeover

by **POKEY BOLTON**

stow, massachusetts

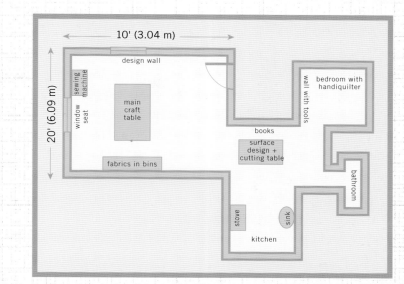

The floor plan includes the following labels: 10' (3.04 m), 20' (6.09 m), design wall, sewing machine, window seat, main craft table, fabrics in bins, books, surface design + cutting table, wall with tools, bedroom with handiquilter, bathroom, stove, sink, kitchen.

before

As my artistic interests have grown and developed over time, so has my stash of tools and supplies—so much so that as the years passed, my studio was morphing into what looked to be a giant compost heap (not an attractive sight). Finding anything became a trial, and many evenings when I came home from work, I'd switch on the light in my studio only to shudder at the illuminated mess before me. In addition to using the space poorly, I had also outgrown all of my ill-suited storage systems. Last year I finally faced the ugly truth: my studio was a dysfunctional mess and in critical need of an organizational—and decorative—makeover.

STUDIO NEEDS CHECKLIST:

Sewing machine table

General craft table

Cutting and dyeing table

Design wall

Ironing table

Area for computer and printer

Area for needle-felting machine

storage for:

Fabric

Stamps

Inks, paints

Paintbrushes

Gels

Cutting mats, rulers, and rotary cutters

Papers

Buttons, ephemera, trims, and embellishments

Threads and yarns

studio needs

The space available to me for a home studio is an in-law unit above my garage that consists of an L-shaped room and a kitchen. I spent several months thinking about the amenities and limitations of my space, what furniture pieces and art items I wanted to keep, and what I could pitch or give away. As I contemplated a newly designed space, I spent a few hours over the course of a week sitting in my cluttered studio with a journal in hand, jotting down notes such as where I usually like to sit, where I like to sew, what wall gets the best light, and what materials no longer hold interest for me. I then drew a blueprint of my space in my journal and placed the various pieces of furniture and working areas where I hoped ideally they could be stationed.

general set-up

In my original studio layout—as messy as it was—I had the bare bones right. I knew I wanted an area dedicated to sewing and general crafts and a second area for cutting and dyeing fabric. Hence I wanted one primary, all-purpose table centrally located, with a second table—mostly used for cutting fabrics and, at times, low-water immersion dyeing—placed closest to the kitchen.

To determine where my design wall would be best situated, I took into account the time of day I'm usually in my studio and which wall receives the best light during that time period. Once my tables and design wall were assigned, I then placed the rest of the important furniture pieces in my blueprint and found they generally stayed in the same locations as my previous space.

color schemes

I wanted a warm and inviting studio space that would set off the artwork, fabrics, and accents within it. I thought about a bold color, but instead chose a warm, yet neutral, taupe for the walls and white tables and shelving to bring more light into the space.

Some people may wonder why someone who paints frequently would choose white for the tabletops. I considered a metal tabletop or even a darker wood; however, for me the white tabletops bring a lightness to my studio that I hope will help me wade through the long New England winters. I make a habit of cleaning my tables

before

before

every time I am done with an activity—a quick squirt of cleaning fluid and a swipe with a rag, and it's ready for its next activity. I also have a stash of recycled newspapers that I use to cover my tabletops when I know I'm going to be rather messy.

furniture and tables

After having used folding tables and chairs for nearly a decade, it was definitely time for an upgrade. Since neither my husband nor I is handy with a tool set, I hired the experts at California Closets to help me design furniture and storage systems that would best suit my needs. This was certainly an investment, but I felt the expertise of a professional designer whose job is to engineer effective storage systems was important to create

ALL PHOTOGRAPHS OF MADE-OVER STUDIO
BY LARRY STEIN PHOTOGRAPHY.

a lasting, well-designed space. Betty Byrne, a local California Closets designer, met with me, and we devised a plan for two tables that were about 36" high. Betty immediately pointed out that the space underneath my old folding table could have been used for storage. Having new tables that were 6" higher than my existing folding tables meant that much more storage space would be available.

Each of my new tables has open shelving for bins and also a set of drawers, some with built-in dividers to help organize the contents. The back of my all-purpose table came with shelving, but I removed the shelves to use my storage system from my previous studio: stackable, clear plastic bins that hold my rubber stamps, inks, die cuts, and other mixed-media tools.

My second table, which I've designated for cutting fabrics and wet work, has a specially designed vertical slot where I can store large cutting mats and quilting rulers. It, too, has two drawers with dividers to store and organize rulers, rotary cutting blades, and other cutting and measuring tools.

storage

fabric In my previous studio, I stored fabric in huge bins that I crammed under folding tables against the walls. Initially I thought keeping my fabrics sorted by color in large bins was a good system; I didn't need to spend time folding fabrics but rather could simply toss it into the bins. I thought it wouldn't take me much time to rifle through each bin and find that perfect fabric for a project. However, because these bins were so large, heavy, and deep, I often couldn't find what I was looking for—never mind the fact that these bins were such an eyesore.

Knowing I needed a brand-new system for fabric storage, I thought about how I like to take stashes of fabric to my table to audition for a project. Hence, I wanted a storage system that was movable. One weekend while flea marketing, I found a wall of vintage locker baskets at an antique store, but they were not for sale. I knew a set of these would be ideal for my organizational needs, while also bringing a sense of playfulness and nostalgia to my studio. Off to eBay I went, where I patiently searched for two months before finding a set of vintage locker baskets offered at the right price. During this time, fat quarter by fat quarter, I folded every last bit of my fabric and sorted by color and hue. A benefit to these vintage locker baskets is that they are square, and each fat quarter fits neatly into a quadrant so that each piece appears on at least one corner of each locker basket. Now I can see my entire fabric stash of a color at once (no digging) and see what I'm lacking or have plenty of.

To the left of my vintage locker baskets is my hutch, where I store my yards of fabrics. This includes upholstery and bridal fabrics, sheers, and some of my painted fabric.

paper The bottom of the hutch is used for paper storage. Because papers tend to spill everywhere if they are not contained, I wanted to keep them sorted by type and stored in shallow bins. I waited for a sale on kitchen shelving at a local store and bought a set of shelf bins, then sorted my papers by type: watercolor paper, tissues, canvas, novelty papers, stationery, etc.

artwork Keeping my storage needs in mind, I turned my thoughts to the artwork and accents I wanted people to notice upon entering my space. When you open the door to my studio, your eye is immediately drawn to the opposite corner, and I knew that was the perfect spot to place my vintage mannequin. I wanted her to face the door as if to say, "Come on in!"

I love to surround myself with the works of others; some artwork in my studio was given to me by friends, others I purchased directly from the artist, and a handful of smaller items I purchased on Etsy.com. My prized piece is a quilt that my great-grandmother handquilted many decades ago. Having the artwork of others around me reminds me that even when I'm grappling with my inner critic, I have others who have undergone the same creative struggles and are in my corner rooting for me. ✳

opposite top left: Stackable plastic bins hold rubber stamps, inks, die cuts, and other mixed-media tools.

opposite bottom right: A hutch holds yards of fabrics, including upholstery, sheers, and painted fabric. Vintage locker baskets show off fat quarters, sorted by color and hue.

5 ways to PERSONALIZE YOUR STUDIO SPACE

1 PAINT IT A SIGNATURE COLOR. Who says a studio has to be white? If turquoise inspires you, go ahead and spread it around the room.

2 DECORATE WITH ARTWORK—yours and others'. Surround yourself with your favorite pieces of art for stimulation and inspiration.

3 SHOWCASE YOUR COLLECTIONS. Do you collect typewriters, antique buttons, or Japanese toys? Group them together for graphic appeal.

4 WRITE ON THE WALLS. Apply chalkboard paint to a wall or cabinet and leave messages to yourself ("Have a creative day!"). Draw picture frames with permanent marker. Paint the road to success across a wall.

5 BREAK THE RULES. There are many opinions about what makes a good studio, but there is only one you. Don't create your studio according to what you "should" do, do what works for you.

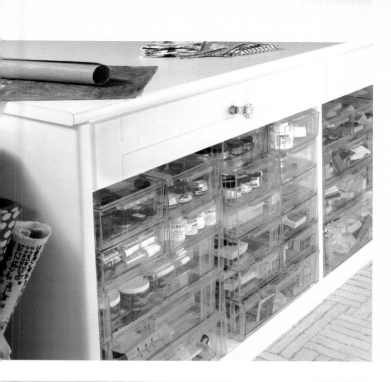

drawn
to design

by **KRISTIN KRAUSE**

cincinnati, ohio

In 2000, my husband and I purchased a four-family historic home in the Gaslight District of Cincinnati, Ohio. We lived in the first floor unit and rented out the other three units. In 2003, the tenant in the second-floor front apartment moved, and we converted that apartment into our master bedroom, a guest room, and a master bath.

GET ORGANIZED:

1 Use chalkboard paint to turn a wall into a changeable drawing board.

2 Contain magazines in standing file boxes covered with journal and doodling pages.

3 Recycle kitchen cabinets and dining room hutches into studio storage. Just paint them for a uniform look.

In 2008, the second floor rear apartment became available. We decided it would become my creative suite—a space for me to create while providing a glitter-free and threadless first floor for my husband, Pete, and dog, Viktoria. I am an avid crafter, creator, designer, and decorator, often working on multiple creative projects at the same time. I wanted my works in progress to have their own unique space, free from the interruptions of our daily lives.

With an extensive schedule of restoration and renovation projects, my studio became my personal renovation project. Since I didn't know how to hang crown molding as my husband has done in other rooms, I chose to draw or paint what I wanted directly on the walls. I wanted to maintain the character of the home while giving it my own modern *trompe l'oeil* twist.

I chose the former kitchen as my studio because of the existing cabinets, sink, built-in shelves, and closet. It is a small space; therefore, the only additional furniture I added to the room was a large 44" × 56" reclaimed table that I covered with vinyl and a vintage hutch that I painted black. Visual clutter is very inspiring to me, and I quickly realized that the stark black of the hutch would feel like I was being forced to create in a cubicle. I removed one of the shelves of the hutch and created an inspiration space that I change regularly to suit the season and/or the nature of my current projects.

My first plan was to draw everything on the walls with a black permanent marker, but I quickly switched to black acrylic paint as it adhered better to the walls, woodwork, and cabinets. The backsplash is painted with

PHOTOS BY KRISTIN KRAUSE AND HANK McLENDON

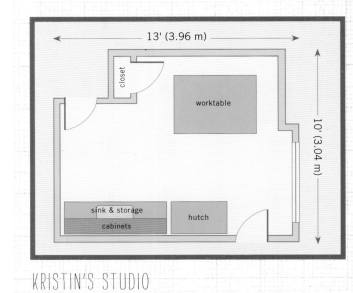

KRISTIN'S STUDIO

chalkboard paint, and the countertop is painted with oil-based paint. The file boxes and suitcases are de-coupaged with writing and doodling pages from my daily journal.

I have thought about creating a children's art gallery for many years and was incredibly inspired by Wes Anderson's movie, *The Royal Tenenbaums* (2001), and the artwork and styling of his brother Eric. I discovered Graham and Brown's Frames wallpaper in a magazine, and I was determined to create my own. My sister's children donated most of the artwork, with a few pieces from other family members and friends. I have been doodling with black Sharpie markers for as long as I can remember, so it was natural to use my doodles as decorative elements throughout the room.

My chalkboard gallery changes frequently and currently features artwork from friends I've met on Flickr. Flickr groups are a great source of inspiration for me. I've discovered many amazingly talented people throughout the world in my Flickr groups.

If you visit me again, you'll see the sitting room portion of my creative suite transformed. ✳

right: A vintage hutch painted black with a shelf removed to allow for a changeable inspiration space (top space in hutch).

opposite: Kristin painted crown molding and other details she envisioned for her creative space.

INSIDE THE CREATIVE STUDIO

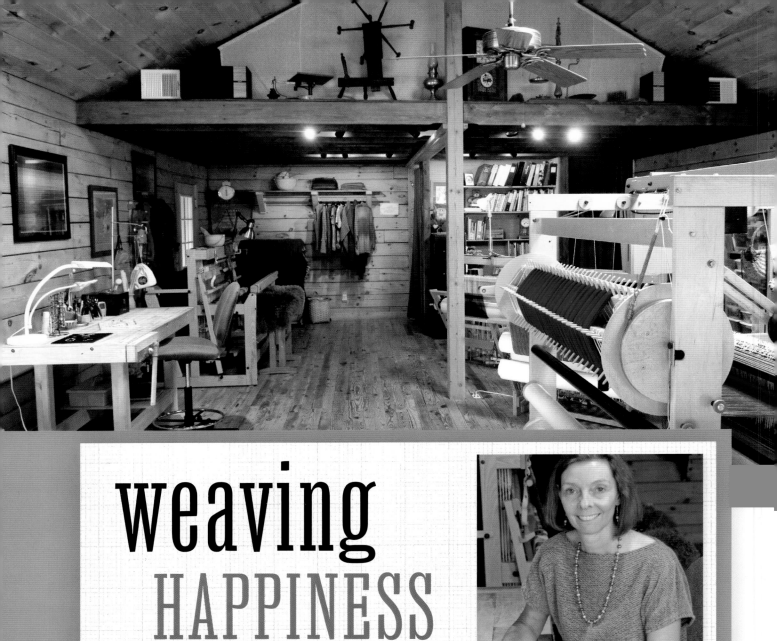

weaving
HAPPINESS
by CHRIS ERICKSON

hanover, pennsylvania

The term I use to describe my art, opalessence, is inspired by the gem, opal. From a distance opals appear white. When you look closely, an iridescent rainbow of color appears. In my weaving, I strive to follow the lesson of the opal. A close inspection of my fabrics reveals they are made from yarns of many colors."

– MARGERY ERICKSON, WEAVER

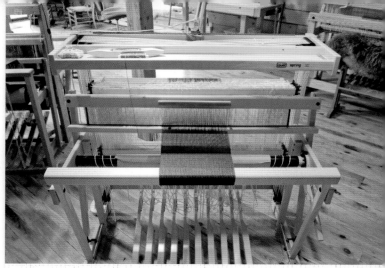

PHOTOS BY ALBERT R. SARVIS

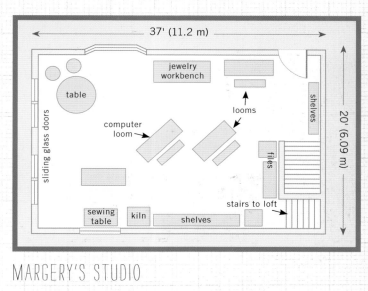

MARGERY'S STUDIO

The studio started as an idea. It was an alternative plan if Margery and I didn't buy a small weaving business and move to New Hampshire. Once the decision to stay put was made, the focus became: what would be needed and how should it look?

design

The space had to hold several looms, a sewing machine desk, and storage for yarn and supplies. A common error, making it too small, was something we wanted to avoid. The first idea, a room 20' × 20', was a bit small; the final size came to be 20' × 35', with a cathedral ceiling, storage loft, and a porch. It would be made from a custom kit put together by the supplier of our log home.

The room would also have a 6' bay window and a pair of sliding glass doors. These provided lots of natural light, brought the outside in, and provided nice views of the yard. The long north wall would have only one

http://user.pa.net/~opal/

One of four looms in Margery's studio.

window, leaving space for yarn and book storage on long shelves.

The loft covers half the room so that creates an additional 20' × 17' storage space. It is actually bigger since we attached the studio to the house with a breeze-way. This is a 10' × 20' outdoor space, covered by the studio roof, connecting the house and studio. The attic over the breezeway extended the loft another 10'.

We enjoy covered porches. With this in mind, the studio has them on three sides, with the breezeway as a fourth.

Finally, because I was going to do the construction, there needed to be just a little more motivation beyond the idea that it was a gift for Marge. I added a basement so there would be more room for my workshop to grow.

The plans were drawn up, sent for review and refine-ment, and the kit arrived in 1994.

construction

Since we had already built our log home, we knew con-structing the studio would not be too big a challenge. However, the weather that summer was wet. It seemed to rain weekly. When it did, construction stopped to al-low the logs to dry out before the next layer went on.

The studio roof had to be attached to the main house. We had to cut into the existing roof and remove shingles. We had serious rain that created a waterfall in the master bedroom. While it was raining and the wind was blowing, I put a 40' × 60' tarp over the roof. We survived, and the water marks on the log walls were sanded off.

completion

The finished studio is beautiful, with lots of natural wood and lots of light. Most of the wood is unfinished pine. The ceiling beneath the loft is stained walnut, giving it a darker contrasting color. The room holds four looms comfortably. Two of the looms can produce cloth 36" wide, one will do cloth 50" wide, and the big one (the size of a four-poster bed and attached to a computer) will do cloth 60" wide. A workbench for jewelry making, a new interest, fits nicely beside the bay window.

So far, the studio has been a classroom for spinners and weavers, an occasional guest room, and a dining area for family picnics. The porches are popular retreats from the heat of the day as well as from the rain and snow.

color is an inspiration

For the past eleven years, Margery has been attending an annual T'ai Chi Chih teacher's conference. Each year, the conference is held in a different part of North America. Returning with renewed energy, she is inspired to weave the color from her trips into her fabric designs. Sometimes it's the warm desert colors from Albuquerque, or the cool, crisp colors of Banff.

In between travels, the changing seasons outside the studio windows provide more color combinations. Thirty-foot pine and spruce trees form a natural boundary, providing a comfortable, secure feeling. A flower garden behind the studio adds new colors each season. At the end of the day you will usually find us on the porch, soaking up the surroundings. ✳

SUN & fun

paint and playfulness let the sunshine in

by JENNIFER HEYNEN

athens, georgia

My studio is a dream come true for me. Being able to walk through my house and up the stairs into this magical space every day is the most amazing commute I could have ever dreamed up.

jangles.net

My biggest challenge was the lack of windows. I hated the idea of not having natural light, but it's a really great space with a door that can be locked. If you have kids, you know why this is important. I chose the brightest and happiest colors I could for the walls to make up for not having windows. I then painted lighter stripes and some flowers on a couple of the walls.

If you are familiar with my work, you know my ceramic beads are pretty much covered in stripes and polka dots. I try to put them on everything, and the studio was no different. My favorite feature in the room is actually the support column that runs from ceiling to floor. I painted it hot pink and orange and then roughed it up a little to look worn; it's eye-catching. I also like the floor; it was painted with cement floor paint. I painted it black with white swirls.

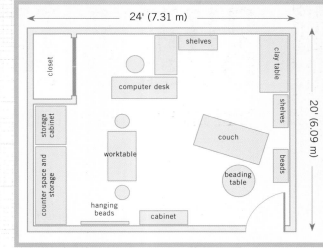

JENNIFER'S STUDIO

A preschool table holds all of Jennifer's beading supplies.

I set up my studio to have stations. When making beads, there are several distinct steps, each of which needs its own table. For instance, when I am making the beads from wet clay, it's pretty messy. Having a table dedicated to this step helps keep the clay dust in one place. I have a big worktable for piling up the project du jour and a computer station for blogging, etc. The best station is my beading table. It's a big round preschool table that has all of my beads and stringing tools on it. It's the height of a coffee table, so I put it in front of my comfy green couch. I love having a couch to sit on while assembling jewelry. If I had to sit in a chair at a desk, I wouldn't be able to work as long.

INSIDE THE CREATIVE STUDIO

A pegboard serves as storage and fun display for strands of beads.

As for storage, there is never enough. I have cabinets along one wall, a pegboard that my strung beads hang on, shelves for boxes of my bead mixes, a metal board for containers of findings, and more. I just brought in another dresser last week for more storage. I hold loose beads in bowls, muffin tins, and metal cookie tins. I love to go to the thrift shops for storage containers. I have picked up several tables and shelves that way, too.

The biggest challenge with my studio has always been keeping it clean. I try really hard to have a place for everything. It's difficult to keep a bead studio looking tidy   ppp because you really need to be able to see the beads to be inspired. If everything is in a drawer, you have to remember what's available to design with. I am always searching for more surface space for the beads. Check back in a few years, and I am sure there will be shelves and tables everywhere. ✳

a window
TO DESIGN

by CATHERINE NICHOLLS

vancouver, british columbia

I have worked in the basement, in a corner of the living room, on the kitchen table, and in a closet—actually in the closet! When we decided to build a larger home, I had the opportunity to design the studio of my dreams.

corvidcreations.net   PHOTOS BY CATHERINE NICOLLS

Our new home sits high on the side of a mountain overlooking Vancouver. While we have a spectacular view to the south over the city, my studio faces north toward the forest. Though I was initially a little disappointed, I get to watch the birds and animals, and north has turned out to be the perfect direction for me. Because of the slope of the mountain, I have a walk-out deck off the back of my second-floor studio and an outside staircase for visitors. It's just a short walk to the vegetable garden, so when I get stuck on a project I can pull a few weeds and wait for inspiration.

The windows in my room face north, west, and east. By choosing to have so many windows, I don't have a permanent design wall, so I have a large curtain rod over the sliding doors to hang up my canvas design wall when I need it. I also tuck bits of inspiration on a bulletin board behind the door or on the wall above

CATHERINE'S STUDIO

top left: Above the sink, open shelving holds paints, mediums, and brushes.

bottom right: The office area contains Catherine's favorite collection—her books.

A stainless steel–topped worktable cleans easily and is the heart of Catherine's studio.

the sink. The floor is stained concrete, making it easy to keep clean. I have a sink and a little built-in fridge. Near the sink I have open shelves to keep all my paints, mediums, and brushes, and some cabinets with doors to hide the really messy things.

There are two areas in my studio—an office area and a work space. The office area also houses my favorite collection: my books. I love books and my studio has shelves running 12' long and 7' high; plenty of space to accommodate the books that had been spread all over in previous homes. There's even room for my jars of shells, feathers, and other precious things.

The work-space area is dominated by a large worktable. After years of trying to find just a few more inches on the counter, I have a worktable that can hold two or three projects at a time. The top is stainless steel and has stood up to everything I have done to it (so far!). It cleans easily, and I think the scratches add character. Under the worktop are roll-out drawers that are about 4" deep. They are the same kind you would have in your kitchen. There's room for my longarm machine, my favorite handstitching chair, and my sewing machine as well.

I love being able to commute to work just up the stairs from the kitchen and, best of all, my four-legged assistant comes with me every day. This really is the studio I have always wanted. ✳

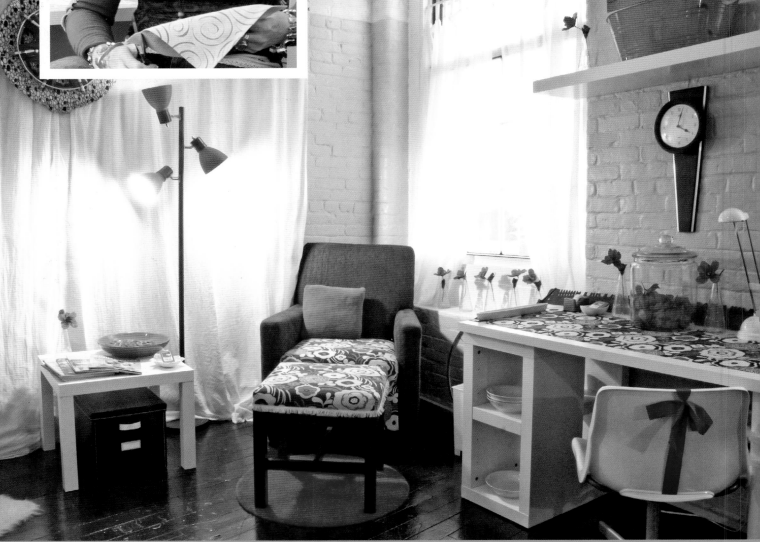

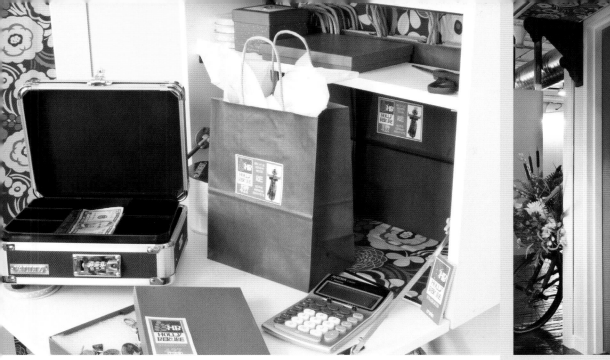

hollyberube.com

what I do: Recycled mixed-media art

why my space works for me: Named "RE," my studio is all about recycle, renew, reuse, and revising. I wanted my space to have a happy, energetic vibe. I purchased most of the storage pieces from IKEA, and then altered them with fabric to make for a more cohesive and inviting space. I decided to split my studio in half to provide a dedicated show space, which is in constant change, while also keeping my workspace my own private cozy retreat. I installed a wall, finished on one side and curtained on the work space side. Initially I had an unsightly utility wall to contend with, but I hung a curtain there also. These curtains conceal bolts of fabric, extra worktables, my wood stash, and cleaning supplies.

When you enter into my studio workspace, you immediately see the 12' high windows, with a view out to the city and train tracks. It's relaxing to listen to the rumbling trains and watch them slowly go by. I placed my easel there by the windows to enjoy the view.

I set up one end of my studio as a social area, with club chairs to relax in. This area works well for meeting with clients, making friends feel welcome, encouraging my teenage daughter to hang with friends, and for me to curl up and look through my favorite books for inspiration. When I need extra work space, I can set up a folding table right over both chairs and make a mess.

The other end of my studio is the real work area. I used good old-fashioned pegboard painted yellow to organize all of my hand tools. The shelving above stores my power tools right where I can grab them, and above that I have placed semitransparent trash receptacles to organize all my supplies. I just take down the receptacle containing the items I need. Below my work space I store my compressor and refrigerator, and on either side I have storage cabinets for paints, fabric, and paper. I also use decorative file boxes to store paper and books. ✷

MY FAVORITE ORGANIZATION PIECE

My "pay and wrap" station. I love this small wall cabinet I got at IKEA, which was called a laptop workstation. I initially got it to house my sewing machine, which it can, but it has turned out to have so many uses. The back of the cabinet has a large rubber band going across to hold your laptop in, but I use it to store all my bags and tissue paper. It also stores a cash box, calculator, scissors, boxes, and ribbon. When I have a sale, I pull the front door open, and it turns into a small table where I can wrap up purchases. My daughter also likes to use it as a dinner table.

Editor: Rebecca Campbell
Art Director: Liz Quan
Designer: Karla Baker
Production: Katherine Jackson

Interweave Press LLC
201 East Fourth Street
Loveland, CO 80537
interweave.com

Printed in China by C&C Offset.

Library of Congress
Cataloging-in-Publication Data

Prato, Cate Coulacos.
 Inside the creative studio : inspiration
and ideas for your art and craft space /
Cate Prato.
     p. cm.
  Includes bibliographical references and
index.
 ISBN 978-1-59668-398-3 (pbk.)
 ISBN 978-1-59668-889-6 (eBook)
1. Handicraft. 2. Workshop recipes. 3.
Artists' studios.
4. Storage in the home. I. Title.
 TT153.P73 2011
 745.5--dc22

2011003667

10 9 8 7 6 5 4 3 2 1

ACKNOWLEDGMENTS

The day that Pokey Bolton, editorial director and founder of *Quilting Arts Magazine* and *Cloth Paper Scissors*, called me into her office to ask if I'd like to take over editorship of *Studios* magazine was the culmination of a lifetime, it seems, of longing. Finally, two of my most favorite occupations—writing and interior design—would come together on an ongoing basis. I can never thank her or Publisher John Bolton enough for that opportunity; the fact that becoming editor of *Studios* led to this book makes it all the more sweet and satisfying.

Help and support along the way have come from every one of my colleagues, but special thanks go to Barbara Delaney, Larissa Davis, Christina Williams, Lindsey Murray, Jenn Mason, Stacey Beaudreau, and Sally Murray. I'd also like to thank my editor on this project, Rebecca Campbell, for her patience and guidance, and for listening.

Most of all, I thank the artists and photographers who opened their studio doors, put artwork on hold while they readied their spaces for photos, and who generously and proudly offered their tips and tricks for storage and organization. I hope their sheer joy at having a studio—big or small, fancy or simple—is evident to all who open this book. Their passion for their creative space is surpassed only by their artistry.

RESOURCES

Furniture and storage

Stackable metal cabinets
bisleyusa.com

Wheeled clothes racks
ikea.com

Wooden, wheeled storage caddies
hinterberg.com

Flat files and other artist storage supplies
dickblick.com and anytimeproducts.com

Hinged plastic containers
The Container Store, containerstore.com, and other storage and organization stores

Archival boxes
lightimpressionsdirect.com

Elfa shelving
containerstore.com

Stainless steel tabletops
ikea.com

Turned wood table legs
tablelegs.com, osbornewood.com, and many lumber yards

Vintage and secondhand
To find local flea markets in your area:
collectors.org/fm/
shopgetorganized.com

Some sources for vintage vessels and other objects to turn into organization and storage pieces:

Brimfield Antique & Flea Market Shows
Brimfield, MA
brimfield.com

Springfield Antique Show & Flea Market
Springfield, OH
springfieldantiqueshow.com/

Alameda Point Antiques and Collectibles Faire
Alameda, CA
antiquesbybay.com

127 Corridor Sale
From West Unity, OH, to Gadsden, AL
127sale.com

Local flea markets, yard sales, eBay, craigslist, and Etsy

Some sources for used store fixtures and displays:
gershelbros.com
storefixturesupercenter.com
Local stores that are going out of business

Cleaning textiles
Linen Wash, linenwash.net.
Soak, soakwash.com.

Supplies for hanging art, fabric, and supplies
Homasote board, homasote.com
Picture rail hanging system, systematicart.com
Clip It Up, clipitup.com.

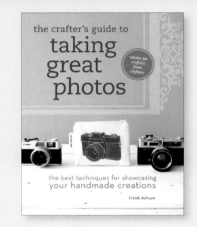